Morning Glories

Also by Sharon Kebschull Barrett

DESSERTS FROM AN HERB GARDEN

Sharon Kebschull Barrett

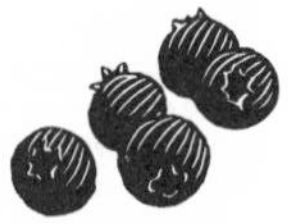

ST. MARTIN'S PRESS NEW YORK

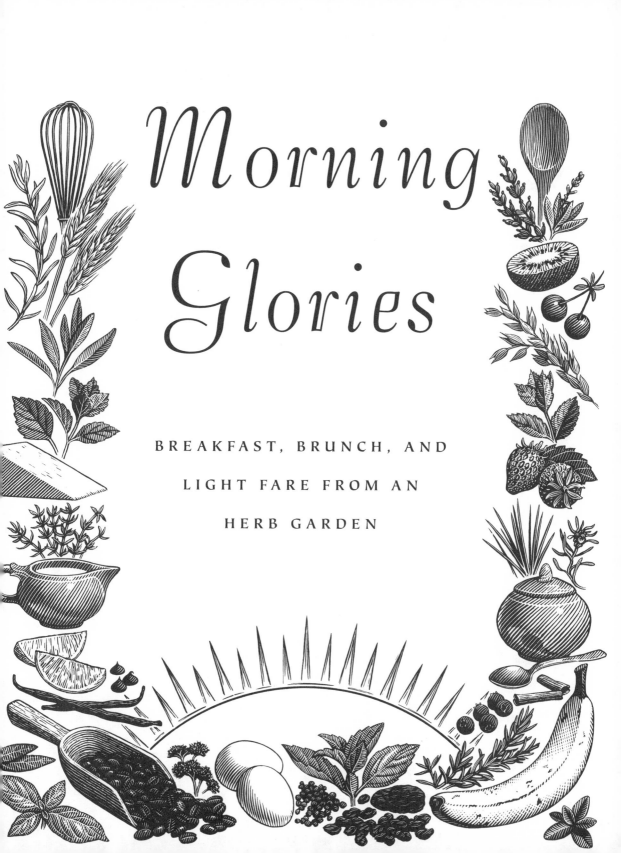

Morning
Glories

BREAKFAST, BRUNCH, AND
LIGHT FARE FROM AN
HERB GARDEN

For Harv and Georgia Kebschull,

with love and gratitude

Book design by Gretchen Achilles

Interior artwork copyright © 2000 by Elizabeth Traynor

Library of Congress Cataloging-in-Publication Data

Barrett, Sharon Kebschull.

    Morning glories : breakfast, brunch, and light fare from an herb garden / Sharon Kebschull Barrett.—1st ed.

      p. cm.

    Includes index

    ISBN 0-312-25224-2

      1. Cookery (herbs) 2. Herbs. I. Title

TX819.H4B37 2000

641.6'57—dc21   00-023030

FIRST EDITION: MAY 2000

10 9 8 7 6 5 4 3 2 1

Contents

Acknowledgments

My cooking career began when I was three years old, at my mother's side. My earliest kitchen memory puts us together in the kitchen making egg salad sandwiches—Mother let me mash the eggs with a pastry blender—and I have rarely been far from the stove since. I am extremely grateful to my parents, to whom this book is dedicated, for allowing me the freedom to experiment, and for at least attempting to eat everything (remember the disastrous shrimp fried rice? and the endless batches of English tea cookies?)! They continue to offer invaluable support in my life.

The rest of my family has also been as supportive and helpful as they were with the writing of my first book. My husband, James, remained patient through all the recipe testing (eggs are great for dinner, but after seven nights of eggs, things start to get a little weird), and all my other strange pregnancy dinners. People constantly tell me how great he is, and I wholeheartedly agree. My sister, Kim Kebschull Otten, again contributed mightily to this book (even as she, too, went through a pregnancy), testing the recipes, doing the index, and offering all the advice and feedback I need—as well as a book title, which I love. And her husband, Mark, and wonderful son, Jonathan, patiently ate their way through this book; my thanks and love to them both. And thank you to Bennett Otten, the newest member of the family, for letting his mother test all this before his birth.

Thanks also go to Debbie Bahl Gessner for her recipe testing and seventeen-year friendship; to Judi and Jim Dingfelder and Kristin and Garry Somers, for their enthusiastic support and tastings; to Marian Lizzi, still a dream of an editor and a genuinely kind person; to my agent, Angela Miller, for her continued support and advice; and to book designers Gretchen Achilles and Krista Olson.

Finally, thanks to someone who had no idea he was being helpful: to Andrew Baxter Barrett, who gave me such joy even before he was born, and who has made our lives richer than we could ever have imagined. To be blessed with Baxter has made life complete.

Introduction

I am completely a morning person. Keep me up all night and I won't be happy about it, but come 7 A.M., I'm Miss Sunshine, ready to greet the day. For me, breakfast is when flavor counts most. No basic cornflakes will do: I want flavors that whisper—and sometimes shout—with a touch of pizzazz and a lot of comfort.

As I discovered with my first book, *Desserts from an Herb Garden,* herbs do magical things for sweets; they can also perk up monotonous mornings. Many of the flavor combinations that work so well in desserts also work wonders in breakfasts. Sweet herbs pair well with fruity drinks (try Orange Mint–Banana Frappe or a Lemon Verbena–Strawberry Smoothie), tender muffins (like Tarragon Cherry Cheesecake Muffins), and sweet and comforting coffeecakes (such as Cinnamon Basil Swirl Cake). Savory herbs—such as marjoram, sage, rosemary, and thyme—that are too often ignored at breakfast go gloriously with all sorts of egg dishes, breakfast puddings, potatoes, and grits.

And it's possible to have a great breakfast or brunch with almost no effort in the morning. For example, make muffin batter ahead, portion it into the muffin cups, and freeze the cups. When your morning needs a muffin, simply bake one, two, or twelve at a time, straight from the freezer, while you shower—they take just five to ten minutes extra in the oven. Rather have scones? Do the same thing: Bake them straight from the freezer. Or how about crisp, flavorful granola to mix into yogurt or eat straight with a glass of milk? It takes just thirty minutes one night to make a week's worth. Need something as fast as that glass of milk alone? Try a quick frappe or chilled fruit soup to drink as you drive. You can even make your own frozen waffles and pancakes.

When you have time, there are more luxurious offerings. Try a Roasted Vegetable Galette, fragrant with oregano and thyme, or Ham and Cheese Breakfast Fondue for brunch. Make sweet yeast breads such as Chocolate, Cranberry, and Lavender Bread, or a Raspberry-Almond Danish Braid to impress your diners. Or try comforting breakfasts of Raised Waffles with Tarragon Strawberry Sauce, Cornmeal Crepes with Lemon Verbena–Ricotta Filling, Bay Rice Pudding with Granola Crunch, or Sweet Potato–Rosemary Waffles topped off with a drizzle of rosemary-infused honey.

Fast or slow, simple or exquisite, decadent or low-fat—*Morning Glories* has you covered, with recipes that bring something new to the table for truly good mornings.

Recipes by Herb

Herbs and Other Ingredients

HERB GARDENING BASICS

Growing herbs can be a massive undertaking, with formal beds requiring meticulous design. Or you can simply plunk some herbs into decent soil in any extra space you have, water them regularly, and ignore them.

I fall—barely—in between those extremes. When I first had the space to plant herbs in the ground, I didn't have the time or resources to make that ground overly attractive. The herbs went in the small plot with the vegetables down the hill, by the street. It wasn't ideal; the garden was never gorgeous, and it was just far enough away to make me lazy about using the herbs in the midst of cooking dinner.

Just before I began writing this book, my husband and I started to remedy that. We've installed a large, three-tier raised bed behind the house, much nearer to the kitchen. I planted lots of flowers, and started my simple herb garden, set like the spokes of a wheel. It still isn't ideal—it doesn't get quite enough sun, so some annual herbs still go down by the veggies, and I use the herbs so often that they have a hard time keeping up with my cutting—but finally, I feel like I'm on the path to being a real gardener.

My early steps (and missteps) on that path taught me a few valuable lessons. First, to get your herbs to thrive, you need to use good soil and ensure good drainage. While it's true that some herbs will do OK in truly sad soil, I want mine to get full and lush, without sacrificing flavor, as fast as possible. We had some good, light soil trucked in to fill the back bed, and the difference has been striking. It was so easy to dig in this soil, unlike our standard clay (even when it's amended with lots of compost and mulch). And the plants seemed happy almost immediately after transplanting, even those that weren't getting quite enough sun.

Also, within reason, ignore books that tell you herbs never need fertilizing. Sure, they'll survive without it, but I found that periodically feeding mine a little weak fish emulsion gives them the kick-start they need when new, or when I've cut them back a tad too far. I don't like to give them too much, though, because that seems to dilute their flavor.

Because I'm a pretty lazy gardener and not inclined to produce formal herb beds, I don't have too many tips for planning your beds. I did, though, make sure to leave space to walk, and I put the perennial herbs in the center so the bed looks decent even after the annuals are shot. And because I'm lazy, I did one other thing to save me tons of time later on: mulch, mulch, mulch. The thick layer of hardwood mulch has meant I have almost no weeds; the light soil means those I do have pull out with ease. It also has made it easy to pull out herbs that get a little too rambunctious, especially mint (while I plant my mints in sunken pots to try to contain them, they still stage periodic garden coups).

In general, grow herbs in soil that is on the alkaline (sweet) side (I dust with a fair amount of lime each year to counteract my acidic soil), usually in full sun to part shade. Use them often for better flavor and vigorous growth. If you're not cutting them often, you'll still need to pinch back any flowers that develop on the annuals to keep them growing. (More often, I cut whole flowering stalks to add to my flower arrangements; a vase of cinnamon basil and anise hyssop flowers with sprigs of pineapple or chocolate mint, plus a touch of citrus sage, is a great bonus from my garden.) Water your herbs in the morning; watering at night may encourage rot.

Most herbs are easy to start from seed, but I buy nearly all mine as small plants— that laziness again, and because I rarely need the amount of plants one seed packet provides. I'd rather fit a greater variety of herbs into my limited space. I am also less inclined than ever to plant such seeds as lime basil or to dig up and bring in tender perennials such as lemon verbena for the winter. In just the past few years, these have become so common that I now easily find reasonably priced plants each spring.

I find virtually all the herbs I could ever want—certainly more than I can fit in—at local nurseries and farmers' markets (the markets are generally a better source than nurseries); see page 151 for a few mail-order sources for extremely hard-to-find plants.

Keep the plants moist when you get them home; I find it's best to leave the pots in the spot where they'll be planted for a day or two of adjustment, to lessen the shock of transplanting. Pinch upright plants such as basil or anise hyssop back by about a third after planting to encourage bushy growth.

I do still keep a pot or two of herbs by my back door, mostly ones I can't ever seem to grow enough of, especially basil. And I grow a few plants, such as bay, in pots to come in for the winter; with a solar house, I have great sun to offer them. However, I usually get frustrated by the time I spend fighting bugs in my house's dry air; using a humidifier helps, but especially for plants such as basil and thyme, I can't ever seem to quite get ahead of the bugs.

That's why this year I tried something new: growing a few potted herbs in my bathroom. We have a large tub under a skylight; I can't think now why I haven't used that space all along. The pots are set in wire racks suction-cupped to the tub's wall, up high enough to avoid the shower spray. They get great sun and the humidity they need; the basil has worked fairly well and not gotten buggy, and the lemon verbena seems quite happy. If you have any similar space, don't waste it!

HERBS USED IN THIS BOOK

Although I can't totally explain why, I simply can't grow lavender; it fails every time. Thus, it's the one herb I don't use fresh in this book. But please *don't use any other dried herbs in these recipes;* you'll always be disappointed. Even oregano, one of the few herbs that's really good dried, tastes better fresh here.

No space or patience to garden? No problem. I've tried to keep this book balanced between specialty and common herbs. Most groceries carry many of my favorites— basil, mint, rosemary, sage, tarragon, and thyme—as well as cilantro, dill, and marjoram.

On the other hand, if you're like me and herbs are a major impulse-buy, soon your garden will be filled with unusual varieties used in none of these recipes. I'm constantly finding new mint and thyme variations, and I love experimenting with them. Be warned, though, that even two varieties of the same herb can have vastly different strengths, so it may take a few tries before the experiment is a success.

Finally, please understand that the following information should be used only as general guidelines for growing herbs; since I live in North Carolina, it's biased toward my experience in hot, humid weather. Especially at farmers' markets, where the seller usually has grown what I'm buying, I always ask for growing tips for my herb purchase (even a common basil or thyme)—I invariably learn something new. (Of course, I'm still waiting for that one magic answer to my lavender questions!)

ALLSPICE *Pimenta dioica:* This is not really an herb, but fresh allspice leaves are too good to resist. The flavor is wonderful, and the plant, which grows slowly into a small tree, is easy to grow in a pot—at least in hot Southern climates—in full sun with rich soil. It must come indoors for the winter.

ANGELICA *Angelica archangelica:* Angelica's height—up to 6 feet, though mine has never come near that—and large leaves make it useful as a center plant for my garden's loosely defined herb wheel (which keeps acquiring spokes as I buy new herbs). Use its leaves whenever you're working with something tart, such as rhubarb or blackberries; while it has a strong flavor on its own, angelica makes your concoction taste sweeter, so you'll need less sugar. It's a hardy biennial; grow it in rich, moist but well-drained soil that is on the acidic side, in sun or part shade; it grows much better in cool climates.

ANISE HYSSOP *Agastache foeniculum:* Many herbs are described as having an anise flavor, including anise, a different (and harder to grow) plant. Anise hyssop and tarragon are my choices for best licorice flavor. A perennial, anise hyssop grows to 3 feet high with lavender-blue flower spikes that are great in casual bouquets. Grow it in full or part sun; it may self-sow. Mine comes back with ease each year; all I need do is remember to pinch it back so I get more than one stalk growing. Don't confuse it with regular hyssop, a bitter herb.

BASIL *Ocimum basilicum:* If it's possible, I fall more in love with basil and its varieties every year. For sweet basil, I prefer the common (Italian) basil with large leaves, which are easier to strip than globe basil's, and lettuce-leaf basil, which tastes great and has enormous leaves. I have also become a huge fan of lime basil and Thai lemon basil, which have some of the most pure lime and lemon flavors available in an herb. Cinnamon basil also offers great flavor and looks gorgeous in the garden or, when it flowers, in floral arrangements. Basil is an annual, easily grown from seed or cuttings. Plant it in full sun in rich, slightly sweet, moist soil—I often add lime to mine. Basil likes the heat and turns to mush at any hint of frost.

BAY *Laurus nobilis:* Take a whiff of a fresh bay leaf and you'll never go back to the dry ones. The scent and flavor are balanced, more nuanced and less bitter in the fresh leaves. Be sure you get true bay, not trees marked as California bay, and grow it in full sun (in hot climates, afternoon shade may be better) in good, well-drained soil. Except in the Deep South, grow it in a pot to bring indoors for the winter. If you simply must use dried leaves, use half the amount of the fresh required in these recipes—but expect the flavor of the dish to be affected.

CHERVIL *Anthriscus cerefolium:* Chervil is a truly delicate herb (add it at the end of cooking so the flavor doesn't fade in the heat) with a wonderful sweet, vaguely anise flavor. It's an annual; grow it in part shade in rich, moist but well-drained soil. It does best in spring and fall, bolting as soon as hot weather hits. Grow it from seed and let it self-sow; if you have patience and space, plant seeds every few weeks for a constant supply.

CHIVES *Allium schoenoprasum:* I love chives, both for their flavor and for the utter ease I have in growing them. These perennials grow to about 10 inches, with pretty, edible purple flowers. They prefer rich, moist soil in full sun to part shade, but mine have done well in less-than-ideal soil. If you have lots, chives are worth cutting and freezing for soups and stews that call for either chives or green onions (scallions). Cut them back after flowering to encourage new growth. Harvest chives by cutting the stalks off at ground level.

CILANTRO *Coriandrum sativum:* This herb is hard to grow in my hot, humid summers, but worth it in spring and fall while it lasts. Cilantro has a soapy flavor people either love or despise (I used to despise it; now I crave it). It's an annual that grows to about 2 feet and needs full sun or part shade and average, well-drained soil. If you have patience and space, plant seeds every few weeks to extend your harvest.

DILL *Anethum graveolens:* An easy and pretty annual with delicate, feathery leaves, dill does best in spring and fall, fading quickly in hot weather. It grows to at least 3 feet in full sun and average to rich, well-drained soil on the acidic side. Cut back the flower heads to keep the leaves growing (and be aware that it reseeds easily). I try to harvest mine when the stalks are still young and fairly soft, so it won't matter if I get a few stalks in with the leaves while chopping.

LAVENDER *Lavandula angustifolio:* Whenever I did signings for my first book, *Desserts from an Herb Garden,* people would tell me how gloriously and easily their lavender grows, and give me tips—and still I can't get it right in my humid summers. But lavender is everywhere now, ever since it was declared the 1999 herb of the year; dried lavender flowers are common in specialty and health-food groceries. A perennial that grows to about 2 feet tall, it needs full sun and average, alkaline soil with very good drainage; it withstands drought once established. *Lavandula angustifolia* is also called English lavender; *Lavandula dentata,* or French lavender, is good as well but must be brought indoors in winter. *Lavandula stoechas,* or Spanish lavender, may do better in humid areas and last the winter. If using fresh lavender in these recipes, use just a pinch more than the amount of dried called for.

LEMON BALM and LIME BALM *Melissa officinalis:* Both balms are sweet but taste slightly medicinal, so I am now much more partial to lemon verbena and lemon and lime basil (especially since these are now quite common at nurseries). But I still appreciate my balms, because they come back each year without any help from me, and they grow fast. With frequent cutting, they make a nice mound about 2 feet tall; should they suffer from neglect, cut them way back—they'll recover nicely. Give them full or part sun (they can even take shade) with average to rich, moist soil; they're hardy perennials that look better if you keep them pinched back (and they self-sow freely, another good reason to keep them under control).

LEMON VERBENA *Aloysia triphylla:* Lemon verbena has definitely become my favorite lemon herb; if only I could get it to grow faster. A tender perennial, it can grow as high as 10 feet; mine usually looks more like a very small bush because I use it so much. It will lose its leaves with any frost, and can only stand temperatures down to about 25 degrees. I sometimes dig mine up and bring it in for the winter, where I let it go dormant, but I'm less inclined to do this these days given how many places now sell nice new plants in the spring. Give it full sun with good, well-drained soil and steady moisture.

MARJORAM *Origanum majorana:* Sweet marjoram has a fuller flavor than that of oregano, and it hints of thyme. It is one of my favorite savory herbs, and can even pair in small amounts with sweet foods. It's a tender perennial that prefers full sun or part shade, in rich, well-drained, alkaline soil; grow it as an annual or try bringing it indoors for the winter. It does better in hot, dry areas, but I've been able to grow enough in North Carolina humidity for my needs without any trouble. You may see another herb labeled hardy sweet marjoram—*O. x majoricum,* or Italian oregano—but it's not as sweet.

MINT *Mentha:* Sure to turn your brown thumb green. Mint makes a great ground cover (so long as you don't mind how it takes over), is super-easy to grow, and offers seemingly limitless varieties for experimentation. My favorites are basic peppermint and spearmint (which you may use interchangeably in these recipes), chocolate mint, lemon mint, orange mint, pineapple mint, and the hard-to-find banana mint. Apple mint is quite common, but I find it very mild, not particularly tasty, and all too invasive for my purposes. A perennial, mint grows as much as 3 feet high—but the problem is the width, not the height. Mint spreads by runners underground, so I often find it sticking up in my garden far from the original plant. It does help to cut the bottom out of its pot, then sink the pot into the ground to contain it a bit, but it still spreads. However, it's easy to pull up and worth growing. Plant it in part shade, although full sun is OK. Mint likes rich, moist soil, but will tolerate average soil. Cut it nearly to the ground if you need a lot (or as winter arrives); it will grow right back.

OREGANO *Origanum vulgare:* Although I like marjoram even better, oregano is a terrific herb and one of the few worth drying. But do taste a leaf before buying a plant, as some varieties have much more flavor (look for subspecies *hirtum,* or Greek oregano). In my garden, oregano grows like a weed to about 2 feet, with no help from me other than to cut back dead stalks occasionally. A perennial, oregano needs full sun, average, well-drained soil, and little else. I've no desire to kill it, but if I did, I'm not sure I could—it's proved that tough. Supposedly it should be divided and replanted every few years so it renews, but I haven't done that yet, and it hasn't slowed a bit. It's also not supposed to like humidity, but mine missed that memo, too.

PARSLEY *Petroselinum crispum:* I always think I should apologize for my indifference to parsley; periodic magazine articles extolling its value make me feel guilty, but I just can't get excited about this herb. I find it a pain to grow in my heat and humidity, and just not worth it when it's so cheap at the grocery store. It's certainly useful as more than a garnish, but I don't tend to create recipes that feature it. Still, it has its place, and I find it especially useful as a filler for pesto if I'm short of basil. I strongly prefer flat-leaf (Italian) parsley. A biennial that's best treated as an annual, parsley grows easily but slowly from seed. Give it full sun to part shade in fairly rich, moist, well-drained soil; fertilize lightly if you cut it back frequently. Harvest the leaves from the outside in, cutting at the base of the stem and leaving as many of the center leaves intact as possible. In hot climates it grows best in spring and fall.

ROSEMARY *Rosmarinus officinalis:* An amazing flavor, versatile for sweet and savory dishes, rosemary is a must-have herb. Around Charleston, South Carolina, where my sister lives, beautiful 6-foot rosemary shrubs are common. People in colder climates will need to grow it in a pot and bring it indoors for the winter. Grow it in full sun in well-drained, slightly alkaline soil. I have a very slow-growing upright rosemary bush; I've had much better luck with creeping rosemary, which grows much faster than its name suggests and is nice along borders. Both produce very pretty pale-blue flowers. It also grows easily from cuttings; I've found that cuttings that have simply been rooted in water will do surprisingly well when potted up.

SAGE and PINEAPPLE SAGE *Salvia officinalis* and *Salvia elegans:* With a strong, slightly musty flavor, sage is a natural with potatoes and savory dishes; it also goes quite well with winter fruits such as apples. Pineapple sage has a good flavor in fruit salads, but the flavor cooks out when heated. Even when used cold, I find its flavor less interesting than pineapple mint, but still good. It also makes a great garnish. Grow sage in full sun in well-drained, average, alkaline soil; it's a perennial that doesn't always like my summer humidity, so some years it comes back better than others. You may also find citrus sage *(S. dorisiana);* I find it useful in the same recipes as pineapple sage.

SALAD BURNET *Poterium sanguisorba:* Burnet's cucumber-flavored leaves are great in salads and a good addition to compound butters; they are also incredibly easy to grow. A 2-foot perennial that easily overwinters (and stays evergreen in warm climates), burnet takes full sun to part shade in average, well-drained soil. It reseeds easily and is one of the few herbs that actually does seem to thrive on neglect; mine gets almost no notice from me and keeps right on growing.

SUMMER SAVORY and WINTER SAVORY *Satureja hortensis* and *Satureja montana:* Summer savory is an annual, while winter savory—my preference for growing—is an evergreen perennial. Summer savory has a more delicate flavor, but if you keep cutting winter savory, it will produce new growth that has an equally delicate flavor—I try to use the leaves that haven't yet turned tough. Both are usually described as tasting something like thyme with a bite, but I find them more akin to rosemary. Winter savory grows low and spreads; summer savory grows to about a foot and then, at least in my climate, flops over and looks distressed at the heat. Winter savory needs full sun and well-drained, average to poor soil; it likes dry, sandy soil just fine but also grows well in richer soils

(I've had some grow quite well in a good soil in a pot with thyme, marjoram, and tarragon). Summer savory needs full sun and light, somewhat rich soil (it will tolerate an average soil).

TARRAGON *Artemesia dracunculus:* Tarragon has proved exceptionally easy to grow in my garden; it just keeps growing despite my inattention. It's a 3-foot perennial that needs full sun to part shade in a very well-drained, rich alkaline soil (it will tolerate sandy soils). Mulch it well in winter. It also grows well in a pot. Be sure to buy French tarragon—which comes as plants only, not seeds—and skip any flavorless Russian tarragon you see.

THYME and LEMON THYME *Thymus vulgaris* and *Thymus citriodorus:* An indispensable herb, for both sweet and savory dishes. There are all sorts of thyme varieties out there, such as caraway thyme and lavender thyme, but the two essentials are common thyme and lemon thyme. Give thyme full sun to part shade and average, well-drained soil; mulch it in winter and cut it back each spring for new growth. It also grows well in containers, so long as you don't water it too much. Make sure you buy common thyme that grows in a small, evergreen, almost-upright plant. Most creeping thymes are too difficult to harvest and strip (although I have two thyme plants that came labeled as creeping thymes that actually have larger-than-usual leaves, making them my favorites).

HARVESTING AND USING HERBS

In general, herbs taste best when cut just before flowering and in the morning after the dew has dried. That's the rule; I rarely follow it. I cut my herbs whenever I need them, and they taste fine. More important than when you cut is how you cut. Never cut back more than a third to half of the plant, and cut whole stems, not just a few leaves off the tops.

If your herbs are dirty, plunge them into a bowl of cold water, swish them around a bit, and let them stand for a few minutes. The grit will drop to the bottom; lift out the herbs and dry them thoroughly—easiest in a salad spinner, OK in paper towels.

To strip small leaves from the stems, hold a stem in one hand at the very top. With the thumb and index finger of your other hand, grasp the stem at the top and run your fingers down the stem; the leaves will strip right off. With large leaves such as basil, however, I generally pluck off groups of leaves just above the stem.

Virtually all the recipes in this book call for minced herbs. They need to be finely minced, so you don't get a big piece of a leaf in any bite. Pile the leaves on your cutting board; they should be very dry, or you'll end up with mush. Hold a chef's knife by the top of the handle, gripping the top of the base of the blade between your thumb and index finger for control. Place your other hand gently on top of the blade for more control and weight. Without ever lifting the tip of the knife from the board, use a rocking motion to chop the herbs until they are in very small pieces—almost to a dust.

There are three standard ways to get herb flavor into your food. You can mix minced or whole herbs in with hot or melting ingredients, to bring out their oils (especially useful if you want to strain out the herb to avoid its texture). You can toss minced herbs with the dry ingredients (be sure the herb is evenly distributed throughout the flour, without clumps, or the flavor won't be right). Or, if you would rather not mince the herbs, you can, in many recipes, grind the whole leaves with some or all of the sugar. A few recipes must be made this way, to bring out enough of the herb's flavor. In other cases, you would not want to grind the herbs because it would give too strong a flavor or create an unpleasant color. But it's usually fine; use your judgment, based on whether the color will show and how strong the herb is to start (I would probably not, for example, do this with rosemary in sweet muffins). To translate the amounts, use twice as many whole leaves, packed, as minced (so 1/4 cup packed whole herb leaves, which is 4 tablespoons, equals 2 tablespoons minced herbs).

Unless the recipe says otherwise, measure your herbs by very lightly pressing them into a measuring spoon or cup—do not pack them down.

OTHER INGREDIENTS AND HINTS

BUTTER: Unsalted butter is best in any kind of cooking, but it's crucial in baking. It lets you control the amount of salt overall, and generally, unsalted butter will be fresher than salted. Salt acts as a preservative and can cover up off-flavors or rancidity, so salted butter can stay on the shelf longer. Avoid it.

BUTTERMILK: When I can find it, I use nonfat buttermilk; more often my markets carry only low-fat buttermilk. Either will work fine in these recipes. In baking, if you can't find it fresh or don't want to buy a whole carton, try using powdered buttermilk (usually stocked in the baking aisle, with powdered milk). Follow the label instructions, mixing the powder with your dry ingredients and adding water where the recipe calls for the buttermilk.

CITRUS ZEST: The zest of an orange, lemon, lime, or grapefruit is just the very outer layer of the peel. Don't get below that top layer; the white part, or pith, is bitter. Grate the zest on a metal box or handheld grater using the smallest round holes available (avoid the extremely small, diamond-shaped holes, as most of the zest gets stuck there and is a pain to clean out). You may also use a vegetable peeler or zester to scrape off the top layer and then mince it with a knife, or run it through a mini food processor for a very fine chop (a coffee grinder set aside specifically to grind spices and herbs—not coffee—also works nicely). If the recipe calls for sugar, add a bit of the sugar to the processor for a better grind.

CREAM: If you can find (and afford) it, look for cream that has been only pasteurized, not ultra-pasteurized. It will whip like a dream (even by hand, it's very quick) and have a fresher flavor, as it has not been taken to the high temperature that ultra-pasteurization requires. Look for it in health-food or gourmet stores. And try to buy heavy cream, not whipping cream, which has a lower butterfat content.

EGGS: All eggs in these recipes are Grade A large eggs. In baking, it's nearly always useful to have the eggs at room temperature, but I rarely have the foresight to pull mine from the refrigerator early. Instead, I place cold eggs in a bowl of very warm tap water for a few minutes, to heat them up just a bit. This isn't so critical for quick breads and muffins, but it can make a difference in yeast breads, preventing a cold shock to the yeast.

FLOUR: When necessary, I have specified a preference for unbleached or bleached all-purpose flour. In general, I prefer unbleached, but since bleached flour is slightly softer, it's a better choice for some tender pastries and biscuits. If you can't get unbleached, bleached will do in all cases. If you have access to soft Southern flours, such as White Lily, use them in the biscuit recipes; they're so soft I often even substitute them for cake flour.

MILK: Unless the recipe specifies, you may use any milk you like—whole, 2 percent, or skim. I drink skim milk, so it's what I bake with when at all possible.

SALT: Please make the effort to search out boxes of coarse (kosher) salt; in some supermarkets they're kept with ethnic ingredients. This, not table salt, is what I use in all my cooking and baking, except for a few times when I prefer the flavor of sea salt. Many chefs prefer coarse salt for its cleaner flavor and the ability to feel the grains between your fingers when you're tossing some into a dish. I strongly recommend cooking with it, but if you prefer to stick with table salt, you'll need to use about one-third less than the coarse salt called for in the recipes.

TURBINADO SUGAR: This is pale, raw sugar. If you can't find it or Demerara, another raw sugar, use granulated sugar or granulated brown sugar instead.

YEAST: Forget those packets of active dry yeast your mother (or grandmother) always used. Look instead for instant yeast, a different strain of the same organism. I use SAF or Fleischmann's brands (see page 151 for sources). I like it because it's totally reliable (I have literally never had a loaf fail to rise since I started using instant yeast), has good flavor, and works vigorously. A package of active dry yeast can contain as much as 25 percent dead cells, and you must mix it with warm water first to see if the yeast bubbles, proving it's still alive; this is the standard first step in most bread recipes. But instant yeast contains more live yeast cells because it's dried at a lower temperature, so it doesn't need proofing first; instead, just mix it with the dry ingredients. (Also, because it has more live cells, you use 25 percent less of it in any recipe calling for active dry yeast—for a standard substitution, use 2 teaspoons instant yeast in place of one envelope of active dry.) Don't use rapid-rise yeast, as it lacks flavor; if you're desperate for time, use a bit more instant yeast for a super-fast rise (but remember that in general a slower rise gives a better flavor). However, if you simply can't find instant yeast, you may use a packet of active dry yeast instead in these recipes, as long as you check the date on the package and know it's as fresh as possible. One final note: Packages of instant yeast often give a very quick expiration date (such as a week past opening, even for very large packages). This assumes the yeast is being used in a hot commercial kitchen. For home use, simply pour it into a zippered, heavy-duty plastic bag and store in the freezer; it will keep fresh for months and should be used directly from the freezer.

Finally, a few random hints that will make these recipes easier and neater:

❖ Whenever I use a cutting board for slicing or mincing, I place a piece of rubbery shelf liner underneath to keep the board from sliding. An old chef trick is to use a wet towel or paper towel, but I find the shelf liner works much better. I also do this under my board when I'm kneading dough or rolling it out.

❖ Whenever I'm using a mixer to beat an ingredient that splatters, especially heavy cream, I drape a towel over the top of the mixer so that it hangs down over the outer edge of the bowl. This catches the splatters quite well.

❖ Instead of greasing my cookie sheets, I use parchment paper. It saves clean-up time and guarantees my food will lift off the sheet without fail. Many kitchen shops and gourmet stores sell the paper in rolls, but I dislike buying it that way (sheets are easier to use) and find it expensive. Instead, see the mail-order source listing (page 151) to order parchment. If you don't want to use parchment paper, lightly grease the sheets instead.

Planning Ahead

Although I'm very much a morning person, I'm not often inclined to cook a lot first thing, even when I have the time. But I don't believe freshly cooked breakfast food should be a luxury, so I've developed a host of quick-fix techniques for those early starts.

Smoothies and breakfast soups can be made the night before and chilled; I prefer to re-blend the smoothies briefly so they're frothy when served. Or, to make and chill the soups quickly in the morning (especially if you didn't start with cold ingredients), simply whisk them over a bowl of ice water.

Some breakfast foods, such as eggs, are easy to prepare at the last minute. Make them slightly faster by mincing the herbs the night before (except for basil, which will turn black and mushy). Other recipes in this book either call for quick cooking or, like the grits, offer do-ahead tips.

Baked goods wouldn't seem as easy to make on short notice, but they are. Here are some preparation and planning tips.

Coffeecakes and Quick Breads

Nothing complicated here—just bake ahead and freeze. Except for the kuchens, all the recipes in this chapter freeze well; I simply wrap them tightly first in plastic wrap, then in aluminum foil. Freeze for up to 3 months. Even the kuchens can be prepped ahead: Make the dough, pat into a rough disk, wrap in plastic, and chill overnight. The next morning, simply press the dough out, top it, and bake.

Remember when you're making any of the coffeecakes or quick breads to follow the recipe's instructions about beating in dry ingredients until barely blended. Keeping these cakes delicate and light is easy so long as you don't overbeat. If in doubt, turn off the mixer and fold the ingredients together by hand, with a rubber spatula.

Muffins, Biscuits, and Scones

This is where you really have some choices in planning ahead. As with the coffeecakes, feel free to bake ahead and freeze, either by double-wrapping in plastic and foil, or by using airtight containers or heavy-duty freezer bags (my preference for muffins and scones).

But there's a better way, one that gives you fresh-from-the-oven morning breads with no work: Freeze the unbaked batter or dough.

For muffins, simply portion the batter into paper- or foil-lined muffin cups and freeze until firm. Transfer the frozen muffins to heavy-duty freezer bags, noting the baking time and temperature on the bag, and freeze up to 3 months (I admit I've gone longer). When you need muffins, simply transfer them back to the muffin tin; no need to thaw. Fill any empty cups in the tin with water to even out the heat in baking. Then bake according to the recipe instructions, adding 5 to 10 minutes as needed to the baking time. That's it—so easy you could even do one or two muffins in a toaster oven, provided you froze them in foil cups (eliminating the need for a muffin tin). It's a wonderful method, especially good when you have company.

The same idea applies to scones: Roll and cut out the scones, then place them on a baking sheet and freeze until solid. Transfer to heavy-duty freezer bags, noting the baking time and temperature, and store up to 3 months. Bake according to the recipe instructions (again, no need to thaw), adding 5 to 10 minutes as needed.

Like the coffeecakes, the trick in making light biscuits, scones, and muffins is to handle the dough as little as possible and/or mix the batters until barely blended.

Yeast Breads

Freezing baked yeast breads works quite well; simply double-wrap them first in plastic, then in foil. Although I freeze unbaked yeast doughs for French bread or pizza, I don't recommend freezing for sweet doughs. You may, however, place a dough to rise (for the first or second rise) in the refrigerator overnight, then continue working with it the next day after letting it come back to room temperature.

The recipes give instructions for mixing and kneading breads by hand or with a hand-held mixer. However, if you own a heavy-duty mixer, feel free to use it—you'll undoubtedly make more bread if you have something else doing most of the work! (For the most part, I avoid food processors for yeast doughs, as I find it too tricky to keep the dough from overheating and overkneading.)

TO USE A HEAVY-DUTY MIXER: Start out with the paddle to mix the ingredients. Then switch to the dough hook to knead; I generally knead on speed 3 of my KitchenAid for about 2 to 3 minutes. I prefer to finish with a minute or so of hand kneading, just to be sure the dough feels right and doesn't get overkneaded.

TO KNEAD BY HAND: Once the dough is somewhat mixed (it will still look lumpy and wet, and some flour may be unincorporated, sticking to the bottom of the bowl), I turn it out onto my lightly floured rolling board and gather it into a rough ball. (I also place a piece of rubbery shelf liner under the board to keep it from sliding as I knead.) With the heel of my right hand, I push down and forward on the top of the dough until it's stretched. With my left hand under the dough, I fold it over my left thumb, pull out my thumb, and turn it 90 degrees clockwise with both hands. Repeat the motions, usually for 5 to 10 minutes, until the dough is smooth, silky, and elastic—pull on it a little to see if it springs back. Note that as I knead, neither hand ever really leaves the dough; it wastes time to keep pulling the left hand back and forth, as my bread-class students are tempted to do. I find these motions fluid and fast.

And *fast* matters. At first you won't be quick, but you'll find the faster you move, the less the dough will stick to the heel of your hand. That, in turn, lets you avoid the temptation to add too much flour, keeping your dough happily moist. You may, of course, need to sprinkle your dough and board with more flour as you go, but *sprinkle* is the operative word here. (After a minute or so of kneading, it may help to clean your hands, as any dough stuck to your hands will continue to stick to the ball of dough.)

If you don't find my kneading method works, you can work out your own motions, so long as you have the push, fold, and turn. Be sure you're pushing away, not just down. Try to work on a counter or table that's a comfortable height (I like ones where, with my arms straight, my palms just rest flat on the counter). If you get a backache quickly, you're at the wrong height.

Once your dough is kneaded or beaten, place it in a clean bowl, and cover it directly with a piece of plastic wrap that's been sprayed or brushed with oil. This keeps the dough from drying out and getting hard, crusty spots that will be unpleasant when they bake. Whenever your dough is rising, keep it covered like this.

Let it rise on the counter at room temperature or, if your kitchen is quite cold, bring a pot of water to a boil and put the water and the dough in a cold oven to create your own moist "proofing box."

Most doughs should rise until they have doubled; to tell when they have, press down lightly with a finger. If the indentation remains and the dough doesn't spring back, it has doubled.

Waffles, Pancakes, and French Toast

Although the instructions for these will always say "serve immediately," there are ways to make these ahead successfully.

If you want to make a whole batch of pancakes, waffles, French toast, or crepes to serve at once, keep them warm by placing them on wire racks set over a baking sheet in a 300-degree oven. Never stack them, as they'll turn flabby. Serve as soon as possible—freshly cooked or close to it will always be best.

Cooked waffles and pancakes (but not French toast) freeze especially well, and I like the luxury of having them available at the last minute (not to mention the high quality, unlike those supermarket frozen versions). Cool them completely, then wrap individually (in plastic) or stack them with sheets of parchment paper or waxed paper in between. Double-wrap them in plastic and foil, or place in a heavy-duty freezer bag.

To reheat frozen waffles, place them in the oven (or in a toaster or toaster oven) at 350 degrees for 5 to 10 minutes, until crisp. They'll crisp better if you place them on a wire rack set over a baking sheet, or even directly on the oven rack.

To reheat frozen pancakes, brush them *very* lightly with melted butter or oil, place on a baking sheet, and heat in a 325-degree oven for about 5 to 10 minutes, until warmed through. (The oil keeps them from becoming rubbery.)

To freeze crepes, stack them as you cook them with a square of parchment paper or waxed paper between each. Wrap the stack in plastic and then in foil, or place in a heavy-duty freezer bag. *To reheat frozen crepes,* thaw overnight in the refrigerator or very briefly in the microwave—just enough to make it possible to separate them. Reheat in the oven at 300 degrees until warmed through.

Cooked waffles, pancakes, and crepes also keep well overnight in the refrigerator, wrapped in plastic; reheat at the temperatures given above just until heated through.

Please do *not* reheat waffles, pancakes, or crepes in the microwave—they'll turn rubbery and unpleasant.

Coffees, Teas, and Other Morning Beverages

Sambuca Latte

Quite simply, I adore this drink—rich, smooth, totally inauthentic as a latte but still delicious.

Even coffee-haters like my husband love it. The directions may look a little long, but it's really

quite quick. Of course, if you have an espresso machine, you may use it instead. You can also

make the syrup ahead and store it in the refrigerator; warm it before using. There may be syrup

left over, depending on your taste—it keeps, chilled, for 2 weeks.

1 tablespoon (packed) minced tarragon leaves

½ cup cocoa (not Dutch-process)

¾ cup water

¾ cup granulated sugar

1 teaspoon instant espresso powder (optional)

1 cup milk (whole, 2 percent, or skim)

3 to 4 cups hot, freshly brewed, strong coffee

1. In a small saucepan, whisk together tarragon leaves, cocoa, water, sugar, and espresso powder until smooth. Set over medium heat and bring to a simmer, whisking; lower heat to medium-low and cook 4 minutes, whisking often. Pour through a fine strainer into a bowl or small measuring cup, pressing on the solids to extract their flavor.

2. Rinse a small saucepan with cold water; shake out but do not dry (this helps keep the milk from sticking and burning). Pour milk into pan and heat over medium heat until hot (or pour into a microwave-safe bowl and heat on high power). Pour into a blender; place a towel over the lid for safety's sake, and turn blender onto high speed for 30 seconds.

3. Put 2 tablespoons of chocolate-tarragon syrup into each of 4 coffee mugs. Divide coffee among mugs; stir well. Divide hot milk among mugs, spooning some of the froth onto each. Serve immediately, adding more syrup if desired.

4 SERVINGS

Minted Hot Chocolate

I make this with skim milk—since it's what I keep on hand—and the larger amount of chocolate to make it super-rich (the corn syrup also gives it a little silkiness). But it's plenty good even with just a little chocolate, for those moments when you need a lift without the guilt.

1. Rinse a small saucepan with cold water; shake out but do not dry (this helps keep the milk from sticking and burning). In pan, whisk together mint leaves and milk. Set over medium-low heat and bring to a simmer. Remove from heat, whisk, and let stand 5 minutes. Pour through a fine strainer into a bowl, pressing on the solids to extract their flavor.

2. Return milk to saucepan; whisk in chocolate chips and corn syrup. Whisk over low heat until the chips are melted and mixture is smooth. Pour into mugs and garnish as desired with mint leaves, marshmallows, or whipped cream.

2 TO 3 SERVINGS

4 teaspoons (1 tablespoon plus 1 teaspoon) (packed) minced chocolate mint or mint leaves

2 cups milk

3 to 6 ounces (½ cup to 1 cup) semisweet chocolate chips

1 tablespoon corn syrup

GARNISH

whole mint leaves, marshmallows, or Lightly Sweetened Whipped Cream (recipe follows) (optional)

Lightly Sweetened Whipped Cream

1 cup heavy cream

2 tablespoons
confectioners'
sugar

1. If you have time, chill a medium bowl and beaters (or whisk, if you're doing this by hand) in the freezer for 20 minutes. Using a hand or stand mixer, beat the cream on low speed for about 10 seconds. Gradually increase to high speed, stopping once to scrape down the sides with a rubber spatula. Beat in confectioners' sugar just as cream begins to stiffen. Beat a total of about 55 seconds for soft peaks and 70 seconds for stiff peaks (this will take several minutes by hand).

2. If not using immediately, transfer to a strainer set over a bowl; cover and chill (excess liquid will drain off; if it gets too thick, whisk in a little more cream).

ABOUT 4 TO 6 SERVINGS

Lemon Verbena Lemonade

A chance remark passed along by my editor led to this lemonade—I couldn't imagine why I hadn't thought of it sooner. Refreshing and different, it's also quick and easy. If you like your lemonade sweet, use the higher amount of sugar. If you want to get fancy, pour a little into an ice-cube tray and immerse whole lemon verbena leaves in the cubes.

1. With kitchen scissors (or use a knife on a cutting board), roughly snip lemon verbena leaves into a small saucepan. Add sugar and 1 cup water; bring to a boil and boil 1 minute. Remove from heat and chill.

2. Strain sugar syrup into a pitcher to remove lemon verbena leaves. Add 2 cups cold water and 1/2 cup lemon juice; whisk well. Taste; add remaining lemon juice as desired. Serve cold.

3 TO 4 SERVINGS

¼ cup (packed) whole lemon verbena leaves

½ to ¾ cup granulated sugar

3 cups cold water, divided

½ to ¾ cup fresh lemon juice

Herb Tea

I have to admit I'm not a huge fan of herb teas, but there are times when they seem wonderfully soothing. My favorites are lemon balm, lemon verbena, and mint teas, but feel free to experiment—and use this recipe just as a guide. I prefer my tea with a spoonful of sugar to round out the flavor, but if you find your tea too bitter to drink without sugar, it means you've steeped it too long. If it needs more flavor, reduce the steeping time and increase the amount of herb leaves.

4 cups cold water

¼ cup chopped herb leaves, such as lemon balm, lemon verbena, or mint

Sugar to taste (optional)

1. Bring water to a boil in a saucepan or tea kettle. As soon as it boils, swirl a little into the teapot to heat it, then pour it out. Add herb leaves to the pot and then the boiling water; cover and let steep 10 minutes. Serve immediately, with sugar if desired.

4 SERVINGS

Sweet Iced Tea

Like good Southerners, we drink a fair amount of iced tea in our house. If it weren't for the amount of sugar in it, we'd certainly drink considerably more—few things quench your thirst better in our sticky heat. Adding a few herbs makes the tea even more interesting without overpowering it: a perfect brunch drink. I lack much of a sweet tooth, but I do like my tea sweet—adjust the sugar to your taste. If this recipe makes more than you want, use 5 tea bags and halve all other ingredients.

1. Place water, sugar, rosemary leaves, lavender, and lemon verbena or lemon balm leaves in a large pot. Cover and bring to a boil over high heat.

2. As soon as water boils, remove from heat and add tea bags (I tie all the strings together into a knot, then drape that over the side of the pan, making sure the bags are submerged). Cover and let steep for 9 minutes. Remove tea bags, pressing gently on them to extract their flavor. Pour tea through a strainer into a pitcher and chill.

I GALLON

16 cups (1 gallon) water

1 ¼ to 1 ¾ cups granulated sugar

2 teaspoons (packed) whole rosemary leaves

1 teaspoon dried lavender

3 tablespoons (packed) whole lemon verbena or lemon balm leaves, roughly torn or snipped with scissors

9 regular-size black tea bags (regular or decaffeinated)

Unsweetened Iced Tea with Herbed Sugar Syrup

I don't like unsweetened tea, and restaurants that think that serving it with packets of sugar and fake sweetener on the side will do are fooling themselves. A better alternative, especially if your house can't agree on sweet tea, is to make a sugar syrup to serve on the side: Granulated sugar on its own won't dissolve in cold tea, but a syrup mixes in well.

SYRUP

1 ½ cups granulated sugar

¾ cup water

¼ cup (packed) lemon verbena leaves, roughly torn or snipped with scissors

¼ cup (packed) lemon mint, orange mint, pineapple mint, or peppermint leaves, roughly torn or snipped with scissors

TEA

16 cups (1 gallon) water

9 regular-size black tea bags (regular or decaffeinated)

1. Make syrup: In a medium saucepan over medium-high heat, bring sugar, water, lemon verbena leaves, and mint leaves to a boil; boil 1 minute. Remove from heat and let cool at least 10 minutes, or to room temperature. Pour syrup through a strainer into a small pitcher or other airtight container; chill.

2. Make tea: In a large, covered pot over high heat, bring water to a boil. As soon as water boils, remove from heat; add tea bags (I tie all the strings together into a knot, then drape that over the side of the pan, making sure the bags are submerged). Cover and let steep for 9 minutes. Remove tea bags, pressing gently on them to extract their flavor. Pour tea into a pitcher and chill.

3. Serve tea with pitcher of syrup on the side.

1 GALLON

Orange Mint–Banana Frappe

I've been making variations of this smooth, froth-topped drink for several years, but it's so much better with the mint, which is a pleasant undertone to the flavors. You can use regular mint, but I prefer the orange mint. If your blender is big enough, this recipe can be doubled.

1. Place bananas, lemon juice, mint leaves, and orange juice in a blender. Process on high speed until bananas and orange mint leaves, are pulverized. With motor running, drop 1 ice cube at a time through the lid opening, and process until ice cubes are crushed (you shouldn't hear any ice chips still being chopped).

2. Pour into glasses and serve immediately, garnishing with mint leaves.

2 SERVINGS

2 ripe bananas, peeled

1 tablespoon fresh lemon juice

2 tablespoons (loosely packed) whole orange mint leaves

1½ cups orange juice

4 ice cubes

GARNISH

whole orange mint leaves

Raspberry–Mint Cooler

This is wonderful for a breakfast on-the-go, especially on a hot summer day. The frozen berries

thicken the drinks (and their cost, unlike fresh, makes it possible to serve this on a regular

basis). I don't mind the seeds here, but pass the cooler through a fine strainer if they annoy you.

¾ cup orange juice

1 tablespoon fresh
   lemon juice

2 tablespoons
   (packed) whole
   mint leaves

3 cups low-fat vanilla
   yogurt

8 ounces frozen
   raspberries

GARNISH

whole mint leaves;
   fresh raspberries
   (optional)

1. Place orange juice, lemon juice, mint leaves, yogurt, and raspberries in a blender, in that order. Blend on high speed until smooth and thick. If desired, strain to remove seeds; pour into tall glasses and garnish as desired.

4 TO 6 SERVINGS

Lemon Verbena–Strawberry Smoothies

These smoothies are especially pretty, flecked with red and green. Be sure to process them thoroughly for the smoothest texture possible. These are best made with chilled strawberries; you could also make them ahead and chill before serving.

1. Place buttermilk, lemon verbena leaves, vanilla, strawberries, and ⅓ cup of the sugar in a blender. Blend on high speed until smooth and thick; taste, and add remaining sugar if needed. Pour into tall glasses and garnish as desired.

3 TO 4 SERVINGS

2 cups buttermilk

2 tablespoons (packed) whole lemon verbena leaves

1 teaspoon vanilla extract

1 pound strawberries, hulled and halved

⅓ to ½ cup granulated sugar

GARNISH

sliced strawberries; whole lemon verbena leaves (optional)

Peach and Pineapple Sage Smoothies

Speed should be a smoothie prerequisite, I think, so I wanted to skip peeling the peaches for this recipe. Pouring the smoothie through a strainer will get rid of the skins, but it also gets rid of the pineapple sage—so it's important to grind the herb first with the sugar to release its flavor. If you want a slightly more complex flavor, add the almond extract, which makes a great combination—just be sure to use only a few drops, as it's powerful stuff.

¼ cup granulated sugar

½ cup (packed) whole pineapple sage leaves

2 cups vanilla yogurt

1 pound peaches, halved and pitted

2 tablespoons fresh lemon juice, or more as needed

Scant ⅛ teaspoon almond extract (optional)

GARNISH

Pineapple sage sprigs (optional)

1. In a blender or food processor, grind sugar with pineapple sage leaves. Add yogurt, peaches, and lemon juice; process until mixture is smooth and frothy. Pour through a strainer into a pitcher, pressing down on solids to extract their flavor.

2. Taste and adjust lemon juice as needed; whisk in almond extract if desired. Pour into tall glasses and garnish as desired.

3 TO 4 SERVINGS

Lemon Mint–Orange Cooler

Light and fresh, this cooler satisfies my need for creamy food—and it's so easy. If you want to experiment, try replacing the lemon mint with lemon basil, or use 1 tablespoon of each.

1. Place orange juice, lemon mint leaves, buttermilk, and 2 tablespoons sugar in a blender; blend on high speed until smooth. With motor running, drop 1 ice cube at a time through the lid opening, and process until ice cubes are crushed (you shouldn't hear any ice chips still being chopped). Taste and add remaining sugar if needed. Pour into tall glasses and garnish as desired.

3 TO 4 SERVINGS

1½ cups orange juice

2 tablespoons (packed) whole lemon mint leaves

1½ cups buttermilk

2 to 4 tablespoons granulated sugar

1 cup ice cubes

GARNISH

Lemon mint leaves (optional)

Muffins,

Biscuits,

and

Scones

Lavender–Blueberry Streusel Muffins

Plain muffins are fine, but I especially like baked goods with a little crunch, so I add streusel toppings wherever possible. This recipe makes large muffins; be sure to press the streusel down a bit so it doesn't fall off as the muffins rise.

2 cups all-purpose flour

¼ teaspoon coarse salt

2 teaspoons baking powder

½ teaspoon dried lavender

2 cups fresh blueberries (or 1 16-ounce bag frozen, thawed and drained), divided

½ cup milk

½ cup (1 stick) unsalted butter, softened

1 cup granulated sugar

2 eggs

½ teaspoon vanilla extract

STREUSEL

½ teaspoon dried lavender

3 tablespoons granulated sugar

¼ cup all-purpose flour

2 tablespoons unsalted butter, diced

1. Preheat oven to 375 degrees. Place paper or foil muffin cup liners in muffin cups.

2. In a small bowl, thoroughly whisk together flour, salt, baking powder, and lavender; set aside. In another bowl, coarsely mash ½ cup blueberries with a fork or pastry blender. Stir in milk; set aside.

3. In a large bowl, beat butter and sugar together on high speed until light and fluffy. Beat in eggs 1 at a time, beating well after each addition. Beat in vanilla. With mixer on low speed, beat in half the flour mixture, then milk mixture, then remaining flour mixture, beating each addition until barely blended. Gently fold in remaining blueberries. Divide batter among muffin cups.

4. Make streusel: In a small bowl, stir together lavender, sugar, and flour; cut in butter with your fingertips or a pastry blender until mixture resembles coarse crumbs. Divide streusel among muffin cups, pressing down slightly to adhere to batter.

5. Bake muffins for 30 to 35 minutes, until tops are golden and a toothpick inserted in the center of a muffin comes out clean. Remove to a wire rack; cool.

1 DOZEN MUFFINS

Lemon Verbena–Blueberry Muffins

These are lower in fat than many of the muffins I make (I am generally not a fan of low-fat baked goods). Fragrant with lemon and bursting with berries, they're a quick, good, low-guilt treat. For a slightly fancier look, you could sprinkle each muffin top just before baking with about 1 teaspoon granulated sugar. And feel free to use raspberries or blackberries instead of the blueberries.

1. Preheat oven to 375 degrees. Place paper or foil muffin cup liners in muffin cups.

2. In a medium bowl, thoroughly whisk together flour, salt, baking powder, sugar, and lemon verbena leaves; set aside. In another bowl, whisk together egg, milk, oil, and vanilla. Pour over flour mixture and fold in until almost combined. Gently fold in blueberries. Divide batter among muffin cups.

3. Bake muffins for 20 to 25 minutes, until tops are golden and spring back when lightly pressed with a finger. Remove to a wire rack; cool.

1 DOZEN MUFFINS

1¾ cups all-purpose flour

½ teaspoon coarse salt

2 teaspoons baking powder

⅔ cup granulated sugar

2 tablespoons minced lemon verbena leaves

1 egg

⅔ cup milk

½ cup canola oil

2 teaspoons vanilla extract

2½ cups blueberries (if frozen, thaw and drain well)

Key Lime Balm Cheesecake Muffins

These big muffins have a creamy filling that renders butter or other toppings unnecessary. Be sure to grease the top of the muffin tin; you could also skip the paper liners and simply grease the tins, but I prefer the guaranteed release of the liners. I keep a bottle of Key lime juice on hand and prefer its flavor here, but fresh lime juice (from standard grocery-store limes) works fine. The muffins can be served warm or at room temperature; they do not need refrigerating.

FILLING

8 ounces cream cheese

1 tablespoon minced lime balm leaves

3 tablespoons granulated sugar

1 tablespoon lime juice

MUFFINS

2 cups all-purpose flour

½ teaspoon coarse salt

1¼ teaspoons baking powder

2½ tablespoons minced lime balm leaves

½ cup (1 stick) unsalted butter, softened

(Continued)

1. Preheat oven to 375 degrees. Grease top of a muffin tin; place paper or foil muffin cup liners in muffin cups.

2. Make filling: In a medium bowl, beat cream cheese on high speed until smooth. Beat in lime balm leaves, sugar, and lime juice until smooth. Set aside. (Beaters should be scraped with a rubber spatula but don't need to be washed before step 3.)

3. Make muffins: In a medium bowl, thoroughly whisk together flour, salt, baking powder, and lime balm leaves. In a large bowl, beat butter and sugar together on high speed until light and fluffy. Beat in lime juice. Beat in eggs 1 at a time, beating well after each addition (mixture may look curdled). With the mixer on low speed, beat in flour mixture until barely blended.

4. Divide half the batter among muffin cups. Divide filling evenly among cups, then top with remaining batter, spreading gently to cover the filling.

5. Bake muffins for about 20 minutes, until tops are golden and firm in the center. Cool pan on a wire rack for about 10 minutes; remove muffins to rack to cool completely (if they stick to tin, cool a little more and run a thin paring knife underneath tops to loosen). Store in an airtight container.

1 DOZEN MUFFINS

1 ¼ cups granulated sugar

¼ cup lime juice

4 eggs

Tarragon–Cherry Cheesecake Muffins

Like the Key Lime Balm Cheesecake Muffins (page 18), these have a creamy filling plus the bonus of juicy cherries. I use frozen cherries, but canned ones also work fine (as would fresh, if you're lucky enough to find them—and patient enough to pit them!). The muffins should be served warm or at room temperature; they do not need refrigerating.

FILLING

6 ounces cream cheese

1 tablespoon minced tarragon leaves

3 tablespoons granulated sugar

MUFFINS

2 cups all-purpose flour

½ teaspoon coarse salt

1¼ teaspoons baking powder

½ cup (1 stick) unsalted butter, softened

1¼ cups granulated sugar

4 eggs

1 teaspoon vanilla extract

(Continued)

1. Preheat oven to 375 degrees. Grease top of muffin tin and place paper or foil muffin cup liners in muffin cups.

2. Make filling: In a medium bowl, beat cream cheese on high speed until smooth. Beat in tarragon leaves and sugar until smooth. Set aside. (Beaters should be scraped with a rubber spatula but do not need washing before step 3.)

3. Make muffins: In a medium bowl, thoroughly whisk together flour, salt, and baking powder. In a large bowl, beat butter and sugar together on high speed until light and fluffy. Beat in eggs 1 at a time, beating well after each addition. Beat in vanilla. With mixer on low speed, beat in flour mixture until barely blended.

4. Divide half the batter among muffin cups. Divide filling evenly among cups, then cherries. Divide remaining batter among cups, spreading gently to cover the cherries (cups will be very full).

5. Bake muffins for 25 to 30 minutes, until tops are golden and firm in the center. Cool pan on a wire rack for about 10 minutes;

remove muffins to rack to cool completely (if they stick to tin, cool a little more and run a thin paring knife underneath tops to loosen). Store in an airtight container.

1 DOZEN MUFFINS

1 16-ounce bag frozen dark sweet cherries, thawed and drained well on paper towels

Apple–Sage Muffins

These sweet muffins, with a crisp top and just a hint of sage, taste just like fall.

2 cups all-purpose flour

¾ teaspoon baking soda

½ teaspoon coarse salt

1½ teaspoons minced sage leaves

½ cup canola oil

¼ cup buttermilk

1 cup granulated sugar

2 eggs

1 teaspoon vanilla extract

1½ cups diced peeled cooking apples, such as Granny Smith (about 2 small)

½ cup chopped walnuts (optional)

1. Preheat oven to 400 degrees. Place paper or foil muffin cup liners in muffin cups.

2. In a large bowl, thoroughly whisk together flour, baking soda, salt, and sage leaves. In a medium bowl, whisk together oil, buttermilk, sugar, eggs, and vanilla. Pour oil mixture over flour mixture and fold in with a rubber spatula until barely blended. Fold in apples and walnuts until just combined.

3. Divide batter among muffin cups. Bake muffins 20 to 25 minutes, until a toothpick inserted in the center comes out clean. Remove to a wire rack; cool.

1 DOZEN MUFFINS

Lemon Thyme Cream Biscuits

Although I love traditional Southern buttermilk biscuits, I crave cream biscuits even more. They're easier to make and, while not low-fat, definitely less guilt-inducing than the traditional ones. To keep these biscuits light, be sure not to handle them too much. For more lemon flavor, add 1 teaspoon minced lemon verbena leaves or lemon balm leaves, or the grated zest of 1 lemon. Try these with Thyme or Lemon Thyme Herb Honey (page 137).

1. Preheat oven to 425 degrees.

2. In a large bowl, whisk together lemon thyme leaves, flour, sugar, baking powder, and salt. Pour in cream and stir it in gently with a rubber spatula until dry ingredients are just moistened.

3. Turn the dough onto a lightly floured surface and press it together with your hands, very slowly adding more cream if needed to get dough to hold together. Roll or pat dough into a circle ¾-inch thick. Cut into 2-inch or 3-inch rounds with a biscuit cutter or drinking glass; pull the cutter straight up each time—twisting it will make the biscuits rise lopsided. Place biscuits slightly separated on a parchment paper–lined or lightly greased baking sheet.

5. Bake biscuits for 15 minutes, or until lightly browned. Serve immediately, or transfer to a wire rack to cool.

18 2-INCH BISCUITS

2 teaspoons minced lemon thyme leaves

2 cups all-purpose flour, preferably bleached

3 tablespoons granulated sugar

1 tablespoon baking powder

½ teaspoon coarse salt

1¼ cups heavy cream, or more as needed

Sage Buttermilk Biscuits

This makes a wet dough, but be sure not to handle these biscuits too much, to keep them light.

These are ideal with patties of Sage, Thyme, and Apple Sausage (page 119); they're also a good

place to experiment with herbs—try rosemary or chives instead. Using a Southern flour here

really does make a difference, if you can get it (see page 151). These are also delicious brushed

with melted butter when they come out of the oven. In place of the cream of tartar, cornstarch,

and baking soda (which make a homemade, single-acting baking powder that I find tastes less

of chemicals than double-acting baking powder), you may use 4 teaspoons double-acting

baking powder.

1 ½ teaspoons cream of tartar

1 ¼ teaspoons cornstarch

I teaspoon baking soda

4 teaspoons (1 tablespoon plus 1 teaspoon) minced sage leaves

4 cups soft Southern flour, such as White Lily, or bleached all-purpose flour

2 teaspoons coarse salt

(Continued)

1. Preheat oven to 500 degrees.

2. In a large bowl, thoroughly whisk together cream of tartar, cornstarch, and baking soda. Whisk in sage leaves, flour, and salt. With your fingertips or a pastry blender, cut in butter until mixture resembles very coarse crumbs. Pour in 1 ¼ cups buttermilk and stir gently with a rubber spatula until dry ingredients are just moistened; add more buttermilk as needed to create a wet but manageable dough.

3. Turn dough onto a well-floured surface and press together with your hands. Pat or roll dough, using a well-floured rolling pin, into a circle ¾ inch thick. Cut into 2-inch or 3-inch rounds with a biscuit cutter or drinking glass; pull the cutter straight up each time—twisting it will make the biscuits rise lopsided. Place

biscuits slightly separated on a parchment paper–lined or lightly greased baking sheet.

5. Bake biscuits for about 10 minutes, until golden. Serve immediately, or transfer to a wire rack to cool.

1 ½ TO 2 DOZEN BISCUITS

8 tablespoons (1 stick) unsalted butter, cut into 16 pieces

1 ¼ to 1 ¾ cups buttermilk

Sambuca Scones

For my book *Desserts from an Herb Garden*, I created Sambuca Cookies that combined tarragon, coffee, and chocolate; they remain some of my most popular—and they're personal favorites. These scones, with their pretty drizzle of chocolate, are rapidly becoming favorites, too; they were my sister's first craving during her pregnancy.

3 tablespoons (packed) whole tarragon leaves

⅓ cup granulated sugar

2½ cups all-purpose flour, preferably bleached

1 tablespoon baking powder

½ teaspoon coarse salt

½ cup (1 stick) cold unsalted butter, cut into 8 pieces

¾ cup plus 2 tablespoons heavy cream, half-and-half, or milk

2 teaspoons instant espresso powder

1 egg, lightly beaten

½ cup semisweet chocolate chips

1. Preheat oven to 425 degrees.

2. In a food processor, whiz tarragon leaves and sugar until leaves are finely ground. Add flour, baking powder, and salt and process briefly to blend. Add butter; pulse processor until butter is in small pieces (do not overprocess).

3. Transfer mixture to a medium bowl. In a small cup, stir together ¾ cup cream and espresso powder until powder is dissolved. With a rubber spatula, stir cream into flour mixture; add remaining cream if needed to make a soft dough. Turn dough onto a lightly floured board; divide in half. Press or roll out each half into a 6-to-8-inch circle; brush lightly with beaten egg. Cut each circle into 8 wedges. Place wedges, not touching, on a parchment paper–lined or lightly greased baking sheet.

4. Bake scones for 10 to 13 minutes, until golden and slightly firm when pressed. Cool completely on a wire rack.

5. Melt chocolate chips on low power in a microwave, stirring after 30 seconds and again in 15-second intervals until melted, or in a bowl placed over (not touching) a pan of simmering water.

Transfer melted chocolate to a small plastic bag. Snip a very small piece off a corner of the bag; drizzle chocolate from this hole onto scones in a decorative, criss cross pattern. Let chocolate set before serving.

16 SCONES

Orange Mint–Chip Scones

I like scones that are flaky and not heavy or overly rich. The main trick in making scones is not to handle them too much, either when cutting the butter in, so it doesn't get soft, or when mixing in the liquid. Use low-fat milk in these, if you like, but try to avoid skim milk—it hurts the texture.

Peel of 1 small orange, removed in strips with a vegetable peeler (avoid white part underneath orange peel)

2 tablespoons (packed) whole orange mint leaves or chocolate mint leaves

⅓ cup granulated sugar

2 ½ cups all-purpose flour, preferably bleached

1 tablespoon baking powder

½ teaspoon coarse salt

½ cup (1 stick) cold unsalted butter, cut into 8 pieces

¾ cup plus 2 tablespoons heavy cream, half-and-half, or milk

½ cup semisweet chocolate chips

1 egg, lightly beaten

1. Preheat oven to 425 degrees.

2. In a food processor, whiz orange peel, orange mint leaves, and sugar until leaves are finely ground. Add flour, baking powder, and salt and process briefly to blend. Add butter; pulse until butter is in small pieces (do not overprocess).

3. Transfer mixture to a medium bowl. With a rubber spatula, stir in ¾ cup cream; add remaining cream as needed to make a soft dough. Fold in chocolate chips. Turn dough onto a lightly floured board; divide in half. Press or roll out each half into a 6-to-8-inch circle; brush lightly with beaten egg. Cut each circle into 8 wedges. Place wedges, not touching, on a parchment paper–lined or lightly greased baking sheet.

4. Bake scones for 10 to 13 minutes, until golden and slightly firm when pressed. Cool slightly or completely on a wire rack before serving.

16 SCONES

Triple-Lemon Scones

This lemony herb combination works well; the slightly medicinal taste of the lemon balm is balanced by the glorious flavor of lemon verbena, while the lemon thyme adds depth and a slight bite.

1. Preheat oven to 425 degrees.

2. In a food processor, whiz lemon balm, lemon thyme, and lemon verbena leaves with the sugar until leaves are finely ground. Add flour, baking powder, and salt and process briefly to blend. Add butter; pulse processor until butter is in small pieces (do not overprocess).

3. Transfer mixture to a medium bowl. With a rubber spatula, stir in ¾ cup cream; add remaining cream as needed to make a soft dough. Turn dough onto a lightly floured board; divide in half. Press or roll out each half into a 6-to-8-inch circle; brush lightly with beaten egg. Cut each circle into 8 wedges. Place wedges, not touching, on a parchment paper–lined or lightly greased baking sheet.

4. Bake scones for 10 to 13 minutes, until golden and slightly firm when pressed. Cool slightly or completely on a wire rack before serving.

16 SCONES

2 teaspoons (packed) whole lemon balm leaves

2 teaspoons (packed) whole lemon thyme leaves

2 teaspoons (packed) whole lemon verbena leaves

⅓ cup granulated sugar

2½ cups all-purpose flour, preferably bleached

1 tablespoon baking powder

½ teaspoon coarse salt

½ cup (1 stick) cold unsalted butter, cut into 8 pieces

¾ cup plus 2 tablespoons heavy cream, half-and-half, or milk

1 egg, lightly beaten

Linzer Scones

These open-face scones take a little longer to put together than standard ones, but the flavor and unusual appearance make the work worthwhile. They not only look pretty but also allow you to get more raspberry jam into the scone than if you tried to encase it between layers of dough. Don't worry if your biscuit cutters are not quite the same size as mine, so long as you maintain the ½-inch thickness of the rolled dough. (Star-shaped cutters create an especially pretty look.) If you have time, toast the almonds first in a 350-degree oven for about 7 minutes (until just fragrant) to further bring out their flavor; let cool before using. Or try mixing in ½ teaspoon almond extract with the cream for a stronger almond flavor.

3 tablespoons (packed) whole lemon verbena leaves

⅓ cup granulated sugar

½ cup whole or slivered almonds (unskinned almonds are fine)

2 ¼ cups all-purpose flour, preferably bleached

1 tablespoon baking powder

½ teaspoon coarse salt

(Continued)

1. Preheat oven to 425 degrees.

2. In a food processor, whiz lemon verbena leaves with the sugar until leaves are finely ground. Add almonds and process just until nuts are finely chopped. Add flour, baking powder, and salt and process briefly to blend. Add butter; pulse processor until butter is in small pieces (do not overprocess).

3. Transfer mixture to a medium bowl. With a rubber spatula, stir in ¾ cup cream; add remaining cream as needed to make a soft dough. Turn dough onto a lightly floured board. Roll out to a rough circle ½ inch thick. Cut out dough with a floured 2-inch biscuit cutter, cutting rounds as close together as possible. With another cutter, about 1 to 1 ¼ inches wide, cut circles from the centers of half of the 2-inch dough rounds to make rings.

4. Transfer the whole dough rounds to a parchment paper–lined or lightly greased baking sheet; brush the top borders lightly with beaten egg. Top with dough rings, pressing down slightly to seal; brush tops lightly with egg. Repeat rolling and cutting with dough scraps.

5. Divide jam among scone centers. Bake scones for 10 to 13 minutes, until golden. Remove from oven; spread jam gently if necessary so that the area inside top rings is covered. Cool slightly or completely on a wire rack before serving; dust lightly with confectioners' sugar if desired (sugar will melt into jam but remain on dough rings).

20 SCONES

½ cup (1 stick) cold unsalted butter, cut into 8 pieces

¾ cup plus 2 tablespoons heavy cream, half-and-half, or milk

1 egg, lightly beaten

½ cup raspberry preserves, preferably low-sugar

GARNISH

Confectioners' sugar (optional)

Thyme, Apple, and Cheddar Scones

Unlike the previous recipes, these scones aren't sweet, making them a perfect accompaniment to egg dishes.

1 tablespoon (packed) whole thyme leaves

2 tablespoons granulated sugar

2½ cups all-purpose flour, preferably bleached

1 tablespoon baking powder

½ teaspoon coarse salt

½ cup (1 stick) cold unsalted butter, cut into 8 pieces

¾ cup plus 2 tablespoons heavy cream, half-and-half, or milk

1 medium apple, peeled, cored, and finely diced

½ cup grated sharp cheddar cheese

1 egg, lightly beaten

1. Preheat oven to 425 degrees.

2. In a food processor, whiz thyme leaves and sugar until leaves are ground. Add flour, baking powder, and salt; process just to blend. Add butter; pulse processor until butter is in small pieces (do not overprocess).

3. Transfer mixture to a medium bowl. With a wooden spoon or rubber spatula, stir in ¾ cup cream; add remaining cream as needed to make a soft dough. Fold in apple and cheese just until combined. Turn dough onto a lightly floured board; divide in half. Press or roll out each half into a 6-to-8-inch circle; brush lightly with beaten egg. Cut each circle into 8 wedges. Place wedges, not touching, on a parchment paper–lined or lightly greased baking sheet.

4. Bake scones for 10 to 13 minutes, until golden and slightly firm when pressed. Cool slightly or completely on a wire rack before serving.

16 SCONES

Coffeecakes

and

Quick

Breads

Lavender Cherry Kuchen

In my first book, I used my mother's famed kuchen recipe with plums for dessert; the kuchen is equally good for breakfast, here with the tasty combination of lavender and cherries. If you use frozen cherries, be sure they are well thawed and drained—even then, you may have to bake the kuchen a little longer to keep it from being soggy. If you don't own a tart pan, make this in a 9-by-13-inch pan.

1 ¼ cups bleached all-purpose flour

¼ cup granulated sugar

Pinch of coarse salt

½ cup (1 stick) cold unsalted butter, cut into 16 pieces

2 egg yolks

1 tablespoon water

1 pound (about 2 cups) pitted sweet cherries, fresh or frozen, thawed and drained

1 ¼ teaspoons dried lavender or 2 teaspoons chopped fresh, mixed with ⅓ cup granulated sugar

1. Preheat oven to 350 degrees. Butter a 9-inch tart pan (with inch-high sides) and set on a baking sheet.

2. Whisk together flour, sugar, and salt in a medium bowl, or process briefly in a food processor. Cut in butter by hand or by pulsing in processor until coarse crumbs form. Whisk together egg yolks and water and add to flour mixture; stir in and knead gently by hand, or pulse in processor, until dough almost forms a ball.

3. Press dough evenly into bottom and sides of prepared pan. Place cherries on top, either arranging them in neat circles or simply tossing them on in a single layer. Sprinkle evenly with lavender-sugar mixture.

4. Bake for 45 minutes, until cherries are tender and pastry is golden; cool on a wire rack at least 15 minutes before serving. Serve warm or at room temperature.

8 SERVINGS

Tarragon Apple Kuchen

Here's another great kuchen variation, one I made up when my appetite was starting to roar during my pregnancy; I had to get my husband to hide it from me so I didn't eat half in one sitting! If you don't own a tart pan, make this in a 9-by-13-inch pan.

1. Preheat oven to 350 degrees. Butter a 9-inch tart pan (with inch-high sides) and set on a baking sheet.

2. Whisk together flour, sugar, and salt in a medium bowl, or process briefly in a food processor. Cut in butter by hand or by pulsing in processor until coarse crumbs form. Whisk together egg yolks and water and add to flour mixture; stir in and knead gently by hand, or pulse in processor, until dough almost forms a ball.

3. Press dough evenly into bottom and sides of prepared pan. Arrange apple slices, slightly overlapping, in concentric circles over dough, starting from outer edge and working in. Sprinkle with tarragon-sugar mixture.

4. Bake for 65 to 70 minutes, until apples are tender and pastry is golden; cool on a wire rack at least 15 minutes before serving. Serve warm or at room temperature.

8 SERVINGS

- 1¼ cups bleached all-purpose flour
- ¼ cup granulated sugar
- Pinch of coarse salt
- ½ cup (1 stick) cold unsalted butter, cut into 16 pieces
- 2 egg yolks
- 1 tablespoon water
- 1¼ pounds (about 4 small) cooking apples, such as Granny Smith, peeled, cored, and thinly sliced
- 2 teaspoons minced tarragon leaves, mixed with ⅓ cup granulated or turbinado sugar

Cinnamon Basil Swirl Cake

This is based on a recipe I clipped years ago from *Gourmet* magazine; it's one of my most popular catering recipes. Exceptionally moist, with a crunchy top, it's satisfying and comforting.

2 tablespoons minced cinnamon basil leaves

1½ cups all-purpose flour

1 teaspoon baking powder

⅛ teaspoon coarse salt

6 tablespoons unsalted butter, softened

¾ cup granulated sugar

2 eggs

2 teaspoons vanilla extract

1 cup sour cream

1 teaspoon baking soda

SWIRL

⅓ cup granulated sugar

2 tablespoons (packed) light brown sugar

2 teaspoons ground cinnamon

8 TO 12 SERVINGS

1. Preheat oven to 350 degrees. Grease a 10-inch springform pan.

2. In a small bowl, whisk together cinnamon basil leaves, flour, baking powder, and salt; set aside.

3. In a large bowl, beat butter and sugar on high speed until light and fluffy. Beat in eggs, 1 at a time, until fluffy and well blended. Beat in vanilla.

4. In a small bowl, whisk together sour cream and baking soda until smooth. With mixer on low speed, beat half the flour mixture into the butter mixture just until blended. Beat in sour cream mixture, then remaining flour, beating just until blended. Spread into prepared pan.

4. Make swirl: In a small bowl, whisk together granulated sugar, brown sugar, and cinnamon. Sprinkle evenly over batter; swirl into batter with the tip of a knife, being careful not to touch the knife to base of the pan.

5. Bake cake for 40 to 45 minutes, until a toothpick inserted in the center comes out clean. Cool completely (or nearly so) on a wire rack before removing pan side and slicing. Serve warm or at room temperature.

Blackberry–Thyme Crumbcake

When I first tested this, it came out so moist—almost pudding-like—that I thought it needed more testing. After two bites, though, I was hooked, especially with the contrast between the moist cake and the crunchy streusel. Lemon thyme would also work well here.

1. Preheat oven to 375 degrees. Grease and flour a 9-inch springform or cake pan, or coat with Baker's Coating (recipe follows).

2. In a small bowl, whisk together thyme leaves, 1¼ cups flour, and baking soda and salt; set aside. In a large bowl, beat butter and sugar together on high speed until light and fluffy; beat in egg and vanilla. On low speed, beat in half the flour mixture, then buttermilk, then remaining flour mixture, beating each time until barely blended.

3. In a small bowl, toss blackberries with remaining 2 tablespoons flour; gently fold into batter. Spread in prepared pan.

4. Make streusel: In a small bowl, combine brown sugar, butter, and cracker crumbs, cutting in butter with your fingertips or a pastry blender until butter is in very small pieces. Spread over batter.

5. Bake cake for 40 to 50 minutes, until a toothpick inserted in the center comes out with only a few moist crumbs clinging to it. (If streusel darkens too fast, cover pan loosely with foil.) Remove pan to a wire rack and let cool completely before serving.

12 SLICES

1 tablespoon minced thyme leaves

1¼ cups plus 2 tablespoons all-purpose flour, divided

1 teaspoon baking soda

½ teaspoon coarse salt

½ cup (1 stick) unsalted butter, softened

¾ cup granulated sugar

1 egg

1 teaspoon vanilla extract

1 cup buttermilk

2 cups blackberries (if frozen, thaw and drain thoroughly)

STREUSEL

¼ cup (packed) light brown sugar

3 tablespoons cold unsalted butter, diced

1 cup graham cracker crumbs

Baker's Coating

Whenever a recipe calls for greasing and flouring pans, use this instead; simply brush it on the pan with a pastry brush. It virtually eliminates sticking. If you bake often, make a double batch.

1 cup vegetable shortening

1 cup vegetable oil (I use canola oil)

1 cup flour

1. In a medium bowl with an electric mixer, beat shortening, oil, and flour together until smooth (consistency will resemble sour cream). Transfer to an airtight container to store; it does not need refrigeration and keeps indefinitely.

2. To use, brush a thin coating onto pan with a pastry brush.

Cinnamon Basil–Cranberry Coffeecake

This is a terrifically moist coffeecake with a sweet, crunchy top—just what I like. I was testing many of these recipes during my pregnancy, when I was trying to sneak whole wheat flour into my baking. Too often this flour simply doesn't work, providing an unwanted flavor and heavy texture. It was a pleasant surprise to find it worked so well here.

1. Preheat oven to 350 degrees. Grease and flour a 9-inch square pan, or coat with Baker's Coating (page 38).

2. In a large bowl, thoroughly whisk together cinnamon basil leaves, flour, baking soda, salt, and cinnamon. In a small bowl, whisk together oil, brown sugar, and eggs. Pour over flour mixture; fold in with a rubber spatula. Fold in cranberries and pecans. Dough will be crumbly; press evenly into prepared pan.

3. Make topping: In a small bowl, stir together brown sugar, granulated sugar, and cinnamon. Sprinkle over dough; swirl into dough with a knife, pulling knife through about 4 times in each direction.

4. Bake for 35 to 40 minutes, until golden on top and a toothpick inserted in the center comes out clean. Cool at least 10 minutes before serving.

12 SERVINGS

¼ cup minced cinnamon basil leaves

2 cups flour: 1 cup whole wheat flour *and* 1 cup all-purpose flour, *or* 2 cups all-purpose flour

1 teaspoon baking soda

½ teaspoon coarse salt

1 teaspoon ground cinnamon

½ cup canola oil

1 cup (packed) light brown sugar

2 eggs

2 cups cranberries, rinsed, dried, and picked over

½ cup chopped pecans (optional)

TOPPING

⅓ cup (packed) light brown sugar

⅓ cup granulated sugar

½ teaspoon ground cinnamon

Orange–Thyme Cream Cake

Cream cakes make great simple desserts—but they're also terrific for breakfast and brunch.

Moist but light, with an old-fashioned glaze (it reminds me of the glazes pictured in my

mother's 1960s cookbooks), they're a gentle start to the day.

1 tablespoon minced
  thyme leaves

1 tablespoon minced
  orange zest

2 cups bleached all-
  purpose flour

¾ teaspoon coarse
  salt

1½ teaspoons baking
  powder

½ cup buttermilk

1 teaspoon vanilla
  extract

¾ cup heavy cream

3 eggs

1¼ cups granulated
  sugar

GLAZE

1 cup confectioners'
  sugar

1 tablespoon half-
  and-half or milk

4 teaspoons orange
  juice (or more as
  needed)

1. Preheat oven to 350 degrees. Grease and flour a 10-cup Bundt pan, or brush pan with Baker's Coating (page 38).

2. Thoroughly whisk together thyme leaves, orange zest, flour, salt, and baking powder; set aside. In a small bowl or in the buttermilk measuring cup, whisk together buttermilk and vanilla; set aside. In another small bowl, beat cream until stiff peaks form; set aside.

3. In a large bowl, beat eggs on high speed (no need to clean the beaters first) with sugar until thick, about 5 to 10 minutes; batter should fall in a ribbon when the beaters are lifted. With the mixer on low speed or by hand, alternately mix in flour and buttermilk mixtures, beginning and ending with flour. Mix just until combined. Gently fold in whipped cream.

4. Pour batter into prepared pan and smooth the top. Bake for 45 minutes, until the top just springs back when pressed. Cool for 10 minutes in the pan on a rack, then turn cake out onto rack to cool completely.

5. Make the glaze: Whisk together confectioners' sugar, half-and-half, and enough orange juice to make a thick but pourable consistency.

6. Transfer cake to a serving dish and drizzle glaze over it.

12 TO 24 SERVINGS

Tarragon Blueberry Bundt Cake

I love Bundt cakes; they're easy to make and look great with little effort. Because you can get so many servings from one cake, they're also great for a crowd. Be sure the pan is well greased.

4 teaspoons (1 tablespoon plus 1 teaspoon) minced tarragon leaves

2 cups all-purpose flour, preferably bleached

1 teaspoon baking powder

½ teaspoon baking soda

½ teaspoon coarse salt

8 tablespoons (1 stick) unsalted butter, softened

1 cup granulated sugar

2 eggs

1 teaspoon vanilla extract

1 cup sour cream

2 cups blueberries (fresh or thawed)

GARNISH

Confectioners' sugar; fresh blueberries (optional)

1. Preheat oven to 350 degrees. Grease a 10-cup Bundt pan.

2. In a medium bowl, thoroughly whisk together tarragon leaves, flour, baking powder, baking soda, and salt; set aside.

3. In a large bowl, beat butter and sugar on high speed until light and fluffy. Beat in eggs, 1 at a time, until mixture is fluffy and well-blended. Beat in vanilla. With the mixer on low speed, alternately beat in flour mixture and sour cream, beginning and ending with flour mixture and beating just until blended. Gently fold in blueberries with a rubber spatula. Spread batter into prepared pan.

4. Bake cake for 55 minutes to 1 hour, until top springs back when lightly pressed. Let cool 5 minutes in the pan, then turn out onto a wire rack to cool completely.

5. To serve, dust cake (it will be dark) with confectioners' sugar, and mound berries in the center if desired; slice along and/or between the ridge lines.

12 TO 24 SERVINGS

Banana Mint Bread

Since I really like banana mint, I expected to like this combination—but still I was pleasantly surprised by how the mint comes through, more as a cooling aftertaste than a shock of mint. Any plain mint also works well here. You can mash the bananas with a fork or pastry blender; frankly, I just smush it through my clean fingers—a great job for a kid, even better for adults who still like to play with their food!

1. Preheat oven to 350 degrees. Grease a 9-by-5-inch loaf pan.

2. In a small bowl, whisk together banana mint leaves, flour, baking soda, and salt; set aside.

3. In a large bowl, beat butter and sugar together on high speed until light and fluffy, scraping down the sides of the bowl at least once. Add eggs 1 at a time, beating well after each addition. Beat in vanilla and bananas just until incorporated.

4. With the mixer on low speed, add half of flour mixture, then buttermilk, then remaining flour mixture, beating just until blended. Pour batter into prepared pan.

5. Bake for 55 to 60 minutes, until bread springs back when top is lightly pressed with a finger. Remove immediately from the pan and let cool on a wire rack.

16 SLICES

1 tablespoon minced banana mint leaves

1¾ cups all-purpose flour

1 teaspoon baking soda

½ teaspoon coarse salt

½ cup (1 stick) unsalted butter, softened

¾ cup granulated sugar

2 eggs

1 teaspoon vanilla extract

1 cup mashed, very ripe bananas (about 3 medium)

⅓ cup buttermilk

Carrot–Savory Bread

I love carrot cake and carrot bread, at least when they're properly moist. This is a great change

from the classic mixture of carrot and cinnamon.

4 teaspoons (1 tablespoon plus 1 teaspoon) minced winter savory leaves

2 cups all-purpose flour

½ cup (packed) light brown sugar

2 teaspoons baking powder

½ teaspoon baking soda

¼ teaspoon coarse salt

2 eggs

½ cup buttermilk or plain yogurt

2 tablespoons canola oil

1 teaspoon vanilla extract

2 cups (lightly packed) grated carrots

½ cup golden or dark raisins (optional)

1. Preheat oven to 400 degrees. Grease a 9-by-5-inch loaf pan.

2. In a large bowl, thoroughly whisk together winter savory leaves, flour, brown sugar, baking powder, baking soda, and salt. In a small bowl, whisk together eggs, buttermilk, oil, and vanilla. With a rubber spatula, stir egg mixture into flour mixture until barely combined. Fold in carrots and raisins.

3. Transfer to prepared pan; smooth top. Bake for 40 to 45 minutes, until a toothpick inserted in the center comes out clean. Remove bread from the pan and let cool completely on a wire rack before slicing.

16 SLICES

Orange–Rosemary Zucchini Bread

Wonderfully moist, slightly lower in fat than many zucchini breads, and full of flavor—all this in a very simple bread. This bread freezes especially well, and is nice both plain and lightly toasted and spread with cream cheese.

1. Preheat oven to 375 degrees. Grease a 9-by-5-inch loaf pan.

2. In a large bowl, thoroughly whisk together flour, baking powder, baking soda, salt, rosemary leaves, and orange zest. In a medium bowl, whisk together sugar, eggs, egg whites, oil, and vanilla. With a rubber spatula, stir egg mixture into flour mixture until barely combined. Fold in zucchini.

3. Transfer to the prepared pan; smooth top. Bake for 45 to 50 minutes, until a toothpick inserted in the center comes out clean. Remove bread from the pan and let cool completely on a wire rack before slicing.

16 SLICES

1 ½ cups all-purpose flour

1 ¼ teaspoons baking powder

1 teaspoon baking soda

¾ teaspoon coarse salt

1 teaspoon minced rosemary leaves

Grated zest of 1 large orange

1 cup granulated sugar

2 eggs

2 egg whites

⅓ cup canola oil

1 teaspoon vanilla extract

1 ½ cups grated, unpeeled zucchini (about 1 large)

Chocolate–Lime Crumbcakes

I really like the look of these—fancier than a muffin—not to mention the taste, moist and fragrant with lime. If you don't have a mini or full-size food processor in which to grind the leaves and sugar, simply mince enough lime basil to equal 2 tablespoons and whisk it in with the flour (but the lime flavor will not be as strong). If you don't have ramekins, the recipe will fill 9 muffin cups; bake them for 20 to 25 minutes.

¼ cup semisweet chocolate chips

¾ cup all-purpose flour

1 teaspoon baking powder

2 tablespoons cocoa powder

¼ teaspoon coarse salt

3 tablespoons (packed) whole lime basil leaves

½ cup granulated sugar

4 tablespoons unsalted butter, softened

1 egg

1 teaspoon vanilla extract

⅔ cup whole milk or half-and-half

(Continued)

1. Preheat oven to 375 degrees. Grease 6 6-ounce ramekins (measuring about 3 inches across) and place on a baking sheet.

2. Melt the chocolate chips, either by stirring them in a small bowl set over (not touching) a pan of simmering water, or by heating them in a microwave on low power for about 1 minute, stir until fully melted, heating them in additional 15-second increments as needed. Set aside to cool slightly.

3. In a small bowl, thoroughly whisk together flour, baking powder, cocoa powder, and salt. In a mini or full-size food processor, whiz lime basil leaves and sugar until leaves are finely ground. Transfer to a medium bowl and add butter; beat until light and fluffy. Beat in egg and vanilla until well blended. On low speed, beat in half of flour mixture until barely blended, then milk, then remaining flour mixture. Fold in melted chocolate.

4. Make streusel: In a medium bowl, whisk together sugar and flour; cut in butter with your fingertips or a pastry blender until mixture resembles coarse crumbs.

5. Divide half of batter among ramekins. Top with half of streusel, then remaining batter, spreading it to cover streusel. Top with remaining streusel, pressing it down slightly.

6. Bake about 30 minutes, until a toothpick inserted in the middle comes out clean or with just a few crumbs. Cool 10 minutes or more on a wire rack; run a thin knife around the edge of the ramekins to release the cakes. Serve warm or at room temperature.

6 INDIVIDUAL CAKES

STREUSEL

½ cup granulated
   sugar

½ cup all-purpose
   flour

3 tablespoons
   unsalted butter

Fruit Puff Pastries

I really like making quick, crisp "danishes" from puff pastry and topping them with a cheese and fruit mixture. You can use frozen puff pastry, but I prefer the flavor of homemade, plus the control I have over the ingredients. True puff pastry, though, is a hassle to make from home. Instead, I use author Maida Heatter's incredibly easy recipe for a base (*Maida Heatter's Book of Great Desserts*)—for a breakfast pastry, it does just fine. Make the dough at night before bedtime, then finish these in the morning. It's fun to experiment here with the flavor combinations; I recommend pairing pineapple (canned is fine) with basil or mint, and blueberries or blackberries with mint or tarragon. Do not use reduced-fat sour cream.

1 cup (2 sticks) cold
   unsalted butter,
   each stick cut into
   16 pieces

1 ½ cups all-purpose
   flour

½ cup sour cream

4 ounces cream
   cheese, softened

⅓ cup granulated
   sugar

1 tablespoon minced
   basil, mint, or
   tarragon leaves
   (see headnote)

1 egg yolk

(Continued)

1. Cut butter into flour by pulsing in a food processor (or by hand, with a pastry blender or 2 knives) until mixture resembles very coarse crumbs. Transfer to a medium bowl and stir in sour cream with a rubber spatula; knead dough very lightly until mixture just holds together. Form dough into a flat disk and wrap it well in waxed paper or plastic wrap. Chill at least 2 hours or overnight.

2. In a medium bowl, beat together cream cheese and sugar until smooth and well blended, scraping down sides with a rubber spatula. Add herb leaves, egg yolk, and vanilla, and beat until smooth. Set aside.

3. Preheat oven to 375 degrees. On a lightly floured board, roll out dough (it will be stiff) to a ½-inch-thick circle, very lightly flouring dough as needed to keep it from sticking. With a 3-inch-round

cookie cutter, cut out dough circles by pressing down and coming straight back up (if you twist the cutter, the dough will puff unevenly as it bakes). Transfer rounds to a parchment paper–lined or lightly greased baking sheet; re-roll pastry scraps and cut as above.

4. Place a dollop (about 2 tablespoons) of cream cheese mixture in the center of each dough round. Top with pineapple chunks or berries.

5. Bake pastries for 25 to 30 minutes, until golden and crisp. Cool on a wire rack; serve warm or at room temperature. Leftover pastries should be stored in an airtight container; reheat at 350 degrees until warm and crisped, about 5 to 8 minutes.

I DOZEN PASTRIES

½ teaspoon vanilla extract

1 ¼ cups pineapple chunks, blueberries, or blackberries (see headnote)

Tarragon Chocolate Puffs

I set out to create a quick version of French chocolate rolls made with bread or croissant dough. I ended up far from my original intent—but what a great conclusion these are. Rich and flaky, they're wonderful as a brunch accompaniment. This recipe uses the same easy base as the Fruit Puff Pastries; for the chocolate, I use Ghirardelli 4-ounce bittersweet bars, broken along the lines, then in half. Do not use reduced-fat sour cream.

1 ½ cups all-purpose flour

¼ cup minced tarragon leaves

1 cup (2 sticks) cold unsalted butter, each stick cut into 16 pieces

½ cup sour cream

24 1-by-2-inch sticks of bittersweet or semisweet chocolate (about 6 ounces)

1 egg, lightly beaten

GARNISH

Confectioners' sugar (optional)

1. In a food processor, whiz flour and tarragon leaves together briefly to blend (or, if working by hand, whisk them together in a medium bowl). Cut butter into flour mixture by pulsing the processor (or by hand, with a pastry blender or 2 knives) until mixture resembles very coarse crumbs. Transfer to a medium bowl and stir in sour cream with a rubber spatula; knead dough very lightly until mixture just holds together. Form dough into a flat disk and wrap well in waxed paper or plastic wrap. Chill at least 2 hours or overnight.

2. Preheat oven to 400 degrees.

3. Cut dough in half; return one half to the refrigerator. On a lightly floured board, roll out other half into a 12-inch square, keeping dough lightly floured as needed to keep from sticking. Cut into 12 6-by-2-inch strips. Place a chocolate stick on the short end of each strip and roll up into a cylinder. Place cylinders, seam side down, on a parchment paper–lined or lightly greased baking sheet. Repeat with remaining dough. Brush tops of all cylinders lightly with beaten egg.

4. Bake puffs for 20 to 25 minutes, until golden and crisp. Cool slightly on a wire rack; serve warm or at room temperature, dusting lightly with confectioners' sugar, if desired. (Don't dust puffs if you plan to reheat them.) Leftover pastries should be stored in an airtight container; reheat at 350 degrees until warm and crisped, about 5 to 8 minutes.

2 DOZEN SMALL PASTRIES

Lemon Verbena–Poppy Seed Cakelets

More like little chiffon cakes than muffins, these individual cakes are pretty and moist.

¾ cup all-purpose
flour

1 teaspoon baking
powder

Pinch of coarse salt

2 teaspoons minced
lemon verbena
leaves

1 tablespoon poppy
seeds

¼ cup fresh lemon
juice

3 tablespoons canola
oil

1 teaspoon vanilla
extract

3 eggs, separated

Pinch of cream of
tartar

⅓ cup granulated
sugar

GLAZE

1 tablespoon fresh
lemon juice

2 tablespoons
granulated sugar

1. Preheat oven to 325 degrees. Place 6 6-ounce ramekins (measuring about 3 inches across) on a baking sheet.

2. In a large bowl, thoroughly whisk together flour, baking powder, salt, lemon verbena leaves, and poppy seeds. In a small bowl, whisk together lemon juice, oil, vanilla, and egg yolks. In another bowl, beat egg whites on high speed until frothy; beat in cream of tartar. Gradually beat in sugar, beating until stiff peaks form.

3. Whisk lemon juice mixture into flour mixture until well blended; it will be stiff. Whisk in about ¼ cup of beaten egg whites to lighten the mixture, then gently fold in remaining whites. Divide batter among ramekins.

4. Bake cakelets for 20 to 25 minutes, until tops are golden and cakes spring back when lightly pressed with a finger.

5. Make glaze: Whisk together lemon juice and sugar.

6. Brush glaze over tops of warm cakelets. Serve warm, running a thin knife around the edge of the ramekins to release the cakelets.

6 SMALL CAKES

Yeast

Breads

Orange–Thyme Oatmeal Batter Bread

I know yeast breads can be scary to new cooks, and often seem too time-consuming for experienced ones. I hope the breads in this chapter will convince you otherwise—but if you need an easier introduction to yeast breads, batter breads are the ticket. Yeast breads don't get quicker or simpler than this—perfect for fresh bread in the morning, but also moist enough to be made ahead. This bread is especially moist and flavorful, perfect plain or with a simple smear of butter. You can make this with either a hand or stand mixer. Try to use instant yeast (see page xxx)—it makes a noticeable difference.

2½ teaspoons instant yeast, or 1 envelope very fresh active dry yeast

2¼ cups all-purpose flour, preferably unbleached

2½ tablespoons minced thyme leaves

½ teaspoon coarse salt

Grated zest of 1 large orange

2 tablespoons unsalted butter, softened

(Continued)

1. Grease or butter a 9-by-5-inch loaf pan.

2. In a medium bowl, thoroughly whisk together yeast, flour, thyme leaves, salt, and orange zest. In a large bowl, beat butter, brown sugar, oats, water, and orange juice on low speed to blend. Add flour mixture; beat on low speed just to combine. Raise speed to high; beat 2 minutes.

3. Scrape batter into prepared loaf pan and smooth top gently; cover batter with a piece of greased plastic wrap. Set near, but not on, oven; let rise for 20 minutes. Meanwhile, preheat oven to 375 degrees.

4. Remove plastic and bake bread for 30 minutes, until loaf is

golden brown on top and sounds hollow when rapped on the bottom. Remove from pan and let cool on a wire rack before cutting.

1 LOAF

¼ cup (packed) light brown sugar

¾ cup rolled oats

¾ cup very warm tap water (about 120 degrees)

½ cup orange juice, at room temperature

Cinnamon Basil–Raisin Batter Bread

This loaf is great plain or toasted. Brush the top with a little milk just before baking, if you want to give it a light glaze. Be sure to toss the raisins in flour, to keep them separated and from sinking to the bottom. As with the other batter breads, instant yeast (see page xxx) is worth using if you can find it.

2 cups plus 1 tablespoon all-purpose flour, preferably unbleached, divided

3 tablespoons minced cinnamon basil leaves

⅓ cup granulated sugar

2½ teaspoons instant yeast, or 1 envelope very fresh active dry yeast

1¼ cups warm milk (about 120 degrees)

3 tablespoons unsalted butter, softened

1 cup dark or golden raisins

1. Grease or butter a 9-by-5-inch loaf pan.

2. In a large bowl, beat 2 cups flour, cinnamon basil leaves, sugar, and yeast on low speed until blended. Beat in milk and butter on low speed to blend. Increase speed to high; beat 2 minutes.

3. Toss raisins with 1 tablespoon flour and beat into batter on low speed just to combine. Scrape batter into prepared loaf pan and smooth top gently; cover pan with a piece of greased plastic wrap. Set near, but not on, oven; let rise for 20 minutes. Meanwhile, preheat oven to 375 degrees.

4. Remove the plastic and bake bread for 30 to 35 minutes, until loaf is golden brown on top and sounds hollow when rapped on the bottom. Remove from pan and let cool on a wire rack before cutting.

1 LOAF

Chocolate Chip–Basil Batter Bread

Super-moist and rich, this loaf gets eaten in minutes at our house if we're not careful. You may want to brush the top with a little milk just before baking, to give it a little glaze. As in the other batter breads, instant yeast (see page xxx) is worth using if you can find it.

1. Grease or butter a 9-by-5-inch loaf pan.

2. In a large bowl, beat 2½ cups flour, basil leaves, sugar, and yeast on low speed until blended. Beat in milk and butter on low speed to blend. Raise speed to high; beat 2 minutes.

3. Toss chocolate chips with 1 tablespoon flour; beat into batter on low speed just to combine. Scrape batter into prepared loaf pan and smooth top gently; cover pan with a piece of greased plastic wrap. Set near, but not on, oven; let rise for 20 minutes. Meanwhile, preheat oven to 375 degrees.

4. Remove the plastic wrap and bake bread for 35 minutes, or until loaf is golden brown on top and sounds hollow when rapped on the bottom. Remove from pan and let cool on a wire rack before cutting.

1 LOAF

- 2½ cups plus 1 tablespoon all-purpose flour, preferably unbleached, divided
- 3 tablespoons minced basil leaves
- ¼ cup granulated sugar
- 2½ teaspoons instant yeast, or 1 envelope very fresh active dry yeast
- 1¼ cups warm milk (about 120 degrees)
- 3 tablespoons unsalted butter, softened
- 1 cup good-quality semisweet chocolate chips

Sweet Orange, Rosemary, and Cranberry Bread

I love the combination of rosemary and orange, and of both those flavors with cranberries. Raisins work well in place of the cranberries, if you prefer. Although this is a yeast bread, there's no kneading involved, and while the two risings and baking take a little while, there's not much actual work. If you like, you can even set the Bundt pan full of batter in the refrigerator overnight; it will rise slowly and be ready for baking in the morning (bring it to room temperature before baking if possible; if not, it may need to bake a bit longer and may not rise quite as high in the oven).

1½ teaspoons minced rosemary leaves

5½ cups all-purpose flour

2 teaspoons instant yeast, or 1 envelope very fresh active dry yeast

1½ teaspoons grated orange zest

1 cup milk

¾ cup granulated sugar

2 teaspoons coarse salt

(Continued)

1. In a large bowl with an electric mixer (preferably a stand mixer), beat rosemary leaves, flour, yeast, and orange zest briefly to combine.

2. In a medium saucepan, whisk together milk, sugar, and salt; add butter pieces and set over medium heat. Whisk until butter is melted. Remove from heat and whisk in cold water. Test temperature of milk mixture with a thermometer or against the inside of your wrist; it should be no more than 120 degrees, or warm to the touch. If it's too hot, whisk it until it's sufficiently cooled.

3. Add milk mixture to flour mixture; beat on low speed until combined. Beat in eggs 1 at a time until well combined. Scrape

down sides of bowl with a rubber spatula. Increase speed to medium for a stand mixer or high for a hand mixer; beat batter for 2 minutes. Beat in cranberries just until distributed throughout the batter. Cover bowl with a piece of greased plastic wrap and set aside in a warm place until dough is doubled (when doubled, dough will not spring back when a finger is pressed into it).

4. Grease a 10-cup Bundt pan. Stir dough down and pour and spread it evenly into the pan. Cover again with greased plastic wrap and set aside to rise until almost doubled. Meanwhile, preheat oven to 375 degrees.

5. Remove the plastic wrap and bake bread for 35 to 40 minutes, until golden brown. Turn out onto a wire rack to cool.

12 TO 24 SLICES

½ cup (1 stick) unsalted butter, cut into 16 pieces

½ cup cold water

2 eggs

1½ cups dried cranberries

Chocolate, Cranberry, and Lavender Bread

I have liked virtually all the chocolate–cherry breads I've come across, especially ones that are not

too sweet, making them a good partner for cream cheese—try this bread with the chocolate-

lavender spread (page 138). Although I really like dried cherries, I also love dried cranberries, and

they're easier to find (and less expensive, so I can munch on them frequently). The slight tartness

of the cranberries pairs well with the lightly floral taste of lavender and the rich chocolate. The

bread freezes well, and half a loaf makes an amazing bread pudding (see page 93).

2 cups milk, warmed
  to about 115
  degrees

2 tablespoons
  unsalted butter,
  very soft

⅓ cup granulated
  sugar

1 teaspoon coarse
  salt

2 teaspoons instant
  yeast, or 1
  package very fresh
  active dry yeast

½ cup Dutch-process
  cocoa

5½ to 6½ cups
  unbleached all-
  purpose flour,
  divided

(Continued)

1. Put the milk and butter in a large bowl. In another bowl, stir together the sugar, salt, yeast, cocoa, and 4 cups flour; stir into milk mixture with a wooden spoon or a mixer. Stir in enough remaining flour, ½ cup at a time, as needed to form a shaggy, firm, but not dry dough.

2. Turn dough out onto a lightly floured surface and knead for about 8 minutes, until dough is smooth, satiny, and elastic, adding flour as needed (or knead with a mixer's dough hook; see page xxxiv). Flatten dough into a large disk; top with lavender, chocolate chips, and cranberries, and fold dough over to enclose them. Knead just until incorporated.

3. Place dough in a clean, lightly greased bowl, and cover directly with greased plastic wrap. Set aside at a warm room temperature to rise until dough is doubled (when doubled, dough will not

spring back when a finger is pressed into it), about 1 ½ to 2 hours. Meanwhile, grease 2 8-by-4-inch loaf pans.

4. Gently punch dough down and divide it in half. Pat each half into an oval and plump by stretching the sides down and tucking under. Place in prepared pans; again, cover directly with greased plastic wrap and let rise until almost doubled. Meanwhile, preheat oven to 350 degrees.

5. Remove the plastic wrap and bake loaves for 40 to 45 minutes, until they sound almost hollow when bottom is tapped; remove from pans and cool on a wire rack.

2 LOAVES

1 ½ teaspoons dried lavender, crushed with your fingers

¾ cup semisweet chocolate chips

1 cup dried cranberries

Cinnamon Basil Rolls

My mother adapted this recipe from my Grandma Kebschull, a pastor's wife in Nebraska—the original includes such directions as "7 cups flour—the coffee cups in the church basement." Today, we use this fabulous dough for stollen, butterhorn rolls, and pecan rolls; these rolls have a topping similar to the one my mother discovered for her famed pecan rolls. To keep the rolls light, keep the dough moist during mixing to the point that it's too sticky to handle. If you have time, after the first rising is complete, punch the dough down, cover it, and let it rise again until doubled, then continue with the recipe. This improves both the flavor and the lightness of the rolls.

6 tablespoons unsalted butter

¾ cup milk

⅓ cup granulated sugar

¾ teaspoon coarse salt

1¾ teaspoons instant yeast, or 1 package very fresh active dry yeast

3½ to 4 cups all-purpose flour, preferably bleached

3 eggs

(Continued)

1. Make rolls: In a small saucepan, melt butter in about half the milk; add remaining milk and heat or cool as needed to 120 degrees. (Test temperature of milk mixture with a thermometer or against the inside of your wrist; it should be just warm to the touch. If it's too hot, whisk it until it's sufficiently cooled.)

2. In a large mixing bowl, mix sugar, salt, yeast, and 1 cup flour; add milk mixture and beat on low speed until combined. Add eggs 1 at a time, beating well after each addition. Then add remaining flour 1 cup at a time, beating well. Don't let mixture get too stiff— you should end with a very soft dough.

3. Place dough in a clean, lightly greased bowl, and cover directly with greased plastic wrap. Set aside at a warm room temperature to rise until dough is doubled, about 1½ to 2 hours (when

doubled, dough will not spring back when a finger is pressed into it).

4. Meanwhile, make filling: In a small bowl, whisk together cinnamon basil leaves, cinnamon, and sugar; set aside.

5. Make topping: In a small pan or microwave-safe bowl, melt butter. Whisk in water and brown sugar until smooth. Divide between 2 lightly greased 9-inch cake pans or pie plates; set aside.

6. When dough has doubled, gently punch it down and divide it in half. On a lightly floured surface, roll out 1 piece of dough to about a 20-by-8-inch rectangle. Sprinkle half the filling mixture over the dough, leaving 1 inch bare on one long side. Starting at the opposite long side, roll up dough in a tight spiral, pinching the seam to seal it. Cut dough into 12 slices. Place 8 slices around perimeter of 1 pan, on top of the topping, with a cut edge facing up. Place remaining slices in center of pan. Cover with greased plastic wrap; set aside to rise until nearly doubled. Repeat with remaining dough.

7. Preheat oven to 350 degrees. Remove the plastic wrap and bake rolls for 20 to 25 minutes, until golden and barely firm. Using oven mitts and being careful to avoid hot glaze, immediately invert each pan of rolls onto a plate; remove pan. Let rolls cool at least partially before serving. To reheat, wrap loosely in foil and place in a 350-degree oven for about 5 minutes.

24 ROLLS

FILLING

2 tablespoons minced cinnamon basil leaves

1 tablespoon ground cinnamon

½ cup granulated sugar

TOPPING

10 tablespoons unsalted butter

3 tablespoons water

¾ cup (packed) light brown sugar

Apricot—Savory Butterhorn Rolls

These rolls showcase one of my favorite flavor combinations. As with the Cinnamon Basil Rolls (page 62), to keep the rolls light, keep the dough moist during mixing to the point that it's too sticky to handle. I like to use as much jam as possible in the rolls, knowing that some may seep out during baking, even when the rolls are well sealed. They freeze and reheat well.

6 tablespoons unsalted butter

¾ cup milk

⅓ cup granulated sugar

¾ teaspoon coarse salt

1¾ teaspoons instant yeast, or 1 package very fresh active dry yeast

3½ to 4 cups all-purpose flour, preferably bleached

3 eggs, at room temperature

1 tablespoon minced winter savory leaves

1 10-ounce jar (about 1 cup) all-fruit apricot jam

1. In a small saucepan, melt butter in about half the milk; add remaining milk and heat or cool as needed to 120 degrees. (Test temperature of milk mixture with a thermometer or against the inside of your wrist; it should be just warm to the touch. If it's too hot, whisk it until it's sufficiently cooled.)

2. In a large mixing bowl, mix sugar, salt, yeast, and 1 cup flour; add milk mixture and beat on low speed until combined. Add eggs 1 at a time, beating well after each addition. Then add remaining flour 1 cup at a time, beating well. Don't let mixture get too stiff—you should end with a very soft dough.

3. Place dough in a clean, lightly greased bowl, and cover directly with greased plastic wrap. Set aside at a warm room temperature to rise until dough is doubled, about 1½ to 2 hours (when doubled, dough will not spring back when a finger is pressed into it).

4. When dough has doubled, gently punch it down. Return it to the bowl and cover directly with greased plastic wrap; set aside at a warm room temperature to double again, about 45 minutes.

5. Meanwhile, make filling: In a small bowl, whisk together winter savory leaves and apricot jam.

6. When dough has doubled again, gently punch it down and divide it into thirds or quarters. On a lightly floured surface, roll out 1 piece of dough to a 10-inch circle. Cut circle into 8 wedges; place about a heaping teaspoon jam (slightly more if making just 24 rolls) on the center of the wide end of each wedge. Fold the long sides of each wedge in to just overlap the filling, then tightly roll up each wedge from the wide end, sealing in the jam and tucking the narrow ends under the rolls. Place on parchment paper–lined or lightly greased baking sheets, cover with greased plastic wrap, and set aside to rise until nearly doubled, 20 to 30 minutes. Repeat with remaining dough.

7. Preheat oven to 350 degrees. Remove the plastic wrap and bake rolls for 15 to 20 minutes, until golden and firm. Serve warm or at room temperature (if not serving immediately, let rolls cool on a wire rack). To reheat, wrap loosely in foil and place in a 350-degree oven for about 5 minutes.

32 SMALL OR 24 MEDIUM ROLLS

Lemon Thyme Brioches à Tête

As with many of my favorite recipes, this isn't a particularly authentic version of brioche, a French bread rich with eggs and butter. But these rolls with little heads are easy to make, and although you have to wait for the dough to chill and then rise, none of the steps is overly involved. If you don't own fluted brioche tins, try muffin tins instead. The chilled dough can also be used for a loaf: Put dough in a greased 8-by-4-inch loaf pan, cover, and let rise until doubled. Slash top (one slash down the length of the loaf) and bake for 40 minutes in a preheated 350-degree oven. Stale brioche makes great French toast.

2 tablespoons minced lemon thyme leaves

2 teaspoons minced lemon verbena leaves or lemon zest (optional)

2 cups all-purpose flour

1 teaspoon coarse salt

¼ cup granulated sugar

¾ teaspoon instant yeast, or 1 teaspoon very fresh active dry yeast

2 tablespoons milk, warmed to about 115 degrees

3 eggs, at room temperature

(Continued)

1. In a medium bowl, mix lemon thyme leaves, lemon verbena leaves, flour, salt, sugar, and yeast. Mix in milk, then beat in eggs 1 at a time on low speed. Add butter; beat on medium speed 4 minutes. Scrape down bowl with a rubber spatula. Cover dough directly with greased plastic wrap; set aside at a warm room temperature; let rise 1 hour, until puffy. Gently press dough down and chill, covered, at least 4 hours and preferably overnight. Dough will be very firm after chilling.

2. Butter the brioche tins and place on a baking sheet. Remove dough from the refrigerator and divide into 10 or 20 pieces, depending on tin size (when formed, dough should fill tins no more than two-thirds full). With lightly floured hands, roll each piece into a ball on a lightly floured surface. To form heads, place each ball on its side, press down with the side of your hand about two-thirds of the way from what was the bottom of the dough, and roll the dough back and forth to create two connected balls, one

smaller than the other. Turn the dough upright and put in the mold; press with your fingers around the small ball (the head) to indent it into the larger ball.

3. Cover molds with greased plastic wrap and let dough rise in a warm place until doubled, about 2 hours.

4. Preheat oven to 375 degrees. Remove the plastic and gently brush each brioche with egg wash, being careful not to let egg drip down insides of the molds. Bake for 18 to 20 minutes, until shiny and dark golden. Cool 5 minutes in the molds before removing to a rack.

10 3-INCH OR 20 2-INCH ROLLS

10 tablespoons unsalted butter, softened

EGG WASH

1 egg, beaten well

Raspberry–Almond Danish Braids

This recipe has moved pretty far from authentic Danish dough; I began with a quick version of the dough that cuts the butter in with a food processor, then made it even quicker by using sour cream to avoid future "turns." Turning the dough—rolling it out, folding it like an envelope, and repeating the process four or five times—isn't hard, but it doesn't fit an impatient person's schedule. This is a good compromise—not as good as the real thing, but still bound to impress your friends and family. Note that you have to make the dough ahead, but you have a few options for making it fit your schedule. Also, if you're as impatient as I am and don't have time to bring the sour cream to room temperature, you can heat it gently in the microwave (try low power for 15 seconds at a time), stirring, until slightly warmed.

2 ½ cups all-purpose flour

1 ¾ teaspoons instant yeast, or 1 package very fresh active dry yeast

1 teaspoon coarse salt

1 cup (2 sticks) cold unsalted butter, each stick cut into 8 pieces

1 cup sour cream, at room temperature

1 egg

(Continued)

1. In a food processor, briefly process flour, yeast, and salt just to blend. Add butter and cut into flour by pulsing just until mixture resembles very coarse crumbs. (Or, thoroughly whisk together flour, yeast, and salt, then cut in butter with a pastry blender or 2 knives.) Transfer to a large bowl. In a small bowl, whisk together sour cream and egg; stir into flour mixture just until blended (mixture will appear slightly dry). Cover with greased plastic wrap and chill overnight or up to 4 days.

2. In a medium bowl, beat almond paste, preserves, and lemon verbena leaves until very smooth; start on low speed or almond paste will fly everywhere, then increase to high speed. Set aside. Then whisk egg white for the glaze until frothy; set aside.

3. On a lightly floured board, roll chilled dough to a 12-by-18-inch rectangle. Fold dough into thirds like a letter, and turn so closed edge is on your left (like a book). Cut dough in half horizontally; wrap half of dough in plastic wrap and place in the refrigerator. Roll remaining dough to a 10-by-16-inch rectangle; transfer to parchment paper on your work surface. With a short end of dough facing you, spread half the almond paste mixture down the center third of the dough.

4. Using a pizza cutter or paring knife, cut about 12 slanting lines in the dough down each long side of the filling, not cutting completely to the filling. Fold in the resulting strips to cover the filling, alternating strips from left side and right side. Press ends to seal and press gently on braid to straighten, if needed. Repeat with remaining dough.

5. Preheat the oven to 400 degrees. Put braids on parchment paper–lined or lightly greased baking sheets. Brush with beaten egg white and sprinkle with sugar if desired. Let braids rest (not right next to the oven), lightly covered with a tea towel, for 20 minutes.

6. Bake braids for 12 to 15 minutes, until golden and crisp. Transfer on the parchment paper to a wire rack to cool slightly before cutting. Wrap any leftovers well in plastic wrap; they may be reheated in a 350-degree oven until crisped and warm, about 5 to 8 minutes.

FILLING

- 8 ounces (1 can) almond paste
- ¾ cup raspberry preserves, preferably low-sugar
- 1 tablespoon minced lemon verbena leaves

GLAZE

- 1 egg white
- ¼ cup pearl or turbinado sugar (optional)

VARIATION: DANISH PINWHEELS

In step 3, after folding the dough (like a letter), do not divide it in half. Roll it out on a lightly floured surface to a 20-inch square. Cut into 16 5-inch squares. Place about 2 tablespoons fruit filling in the center of each square. With a paring knife, cut a slash from the filling (but don't cut quite to the filling) to each corner. Fold in every other pastry point to the center, overlapping to create a pinwheel. Follow braid instructions from step 5 on, transferring pinwheels to parchment paper–lined or lightly greased baking sheets and brushing exposed dough with egg white before sprinkling with sugar.

12 SLICES

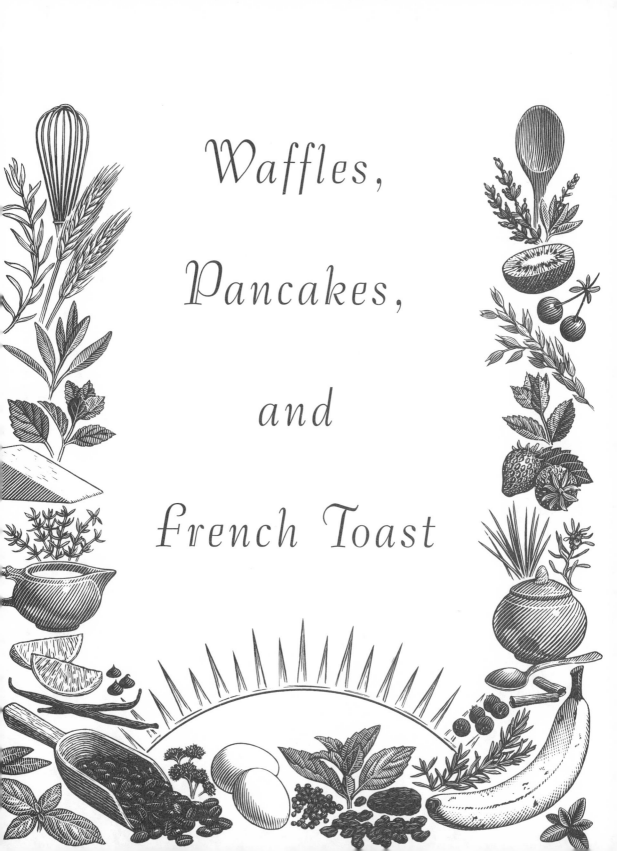

Waffles,

Pancakes,

and

French Toast

Lemon Verbena Waffles

It's great to have one really quick, basic waffle recipe, and this is it. I use this when I'm in a hurry, but if I have just a little more time, I make the Light and Crisp variation with separated eggs—the beaten whites offer more lightness and crunch. You could serve these with a fruit syrup, but I like them best topped with sliced fresh fruit. For something creamy on top of that, try pureeing cottage cheese in a food processor until very smooth, then sweetening it to taste with sugar and vanilla extract. This low-fat idea, from *Maida Heatter's Book of Great American Desserts,* adds just the right finish. Note that the lower herb amount offers just a hint of lemon, good if you don't want too strong a contrast with your topping.

2 cups all-purpose flour

2 to 3 tablespoons minced lemon verbena leaves

1 tablespoon baking powder

2 tablespoons granulated sugar

¾ teaspoon coarse salt

2 eggs

½ teaspoon vanilla extract

2 cups milk

6 tablespoons unsalted butter, melted

1. In a medium bowl, thoroughly whisk together flour, lemon verbena leaves, baking powder, sugar, and salt. Whisk in eggs, vanilla, and milk until combined; whisk in butter.

2. Preheat a waffle iron according to manufacturer's instructions.

3. Ladle waffle batter onto the iron according to manufacturer's instructions, oiling iron first if needed. Cook until iron stops steaming; waffles should be crisp. Serve immediately.

LIGHT AND CRISP VARIATION

Separate eggs. Whisk in egg yolks in step 1 with the vanilla and milk, then whisk in butter. Beat egg whites with a mixer on high speed (or by hand) until stiff peaks form. Fold ¼ of whites into batter to lighten it; gently fold remaining whites into batter just until incorporated. Proceed as above.

10 6-INCH WAFFLES

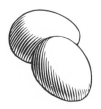

Blueberry–Basil Cornmeal Waffles

I like crispness and crunch in my food, and I really dislike soggy waffles. The cornmeal in these adds to the crunch and pairs well with the blueberries and basil, and with warmed maple syrup poured on top (the real thing, please!—my grandfather used to give us syrup he tapped from his trees in Connecticut, and after that, I could never eat fake syrup with wonderful homemade waffles). You may need to keep the iron well oiled to stop the blueberries from sticking.

3 tablespoons minced basil leaves

1 ½ cups cornmeal

½ cup all-purpose flour

½ teaspoon coarse salt

¼ cup granulated sugar

1 teaspoon baking powder

1 teaspoon baking soda

2 eggs, separated

2 cups buttermilk

1 teaspoon vanilla extract

½ cup unsalted butter (1 stick), melted

1 cup blueberries (if frozen, thawed and drained well)

1. In a large bowl, whisk together basil leaves, cornmeal, flour, salt, sugar, baking powder, and baking soda. In a medium bowl, whisk together egg yolks, buttermilk, and vanilla. In a small bowl, beat or whisk egg whites until stiff peaks form.

2. Preheat a waffle iron according to manufacturer's instructions.

3. Pour buttermilk mixture over cornmeal mixture; whisk well. Add butter and whisk until smooth. With a rubber spatula, gently fold in beaten egg whites, then blueberries.

4. Ladle waffle batter onto the iron according to manufacturer's instructions, oiling iron first if needed. Cook until iron stops steaming; waffles should be crisp. Serve immediately.

10 TO 12 6-INCH WAFFLES

Raised Waffles with Tarragon Strawberry Sauce

This is a great do-ahead recipe. The waffles bake up crisp and golden, with an almost lacy look—but note that they soften fast under the sauce. The recipe is based on one from *The Breakfast Book,* by Marion Cunningham, who based hers on Fannie Farmer's recipe. (Leftover batter may be stored in the refrigerator, tightly covered, for up to 2 days.)

1. In a large bowl, whisk together milk, yeast, butter, salt, sugar, and flour until very smooth. Cover bowl with plastic wrap and refrigerate overnight, or up to 3 days. (If your kitchen is cool, leave the bowl on the counter overnight instead of chilling it.)

2. When you're ready to make waffles, whisk eggs, baking soda, and vanilla into batter (which may look separated); whisk until smooth. (At this point, batter may stand at room temperature up to 30 minutes.)

3. Preheat a waffle iron according to manufacturer's instructions, and oil iron if needed.

4. Ladle waffle batter onto the iron according to manufacturer's instructions; do not overfill. Cook until iron stops steaming; waffles should be crisp. Serve immediately with warm Tarragon Strawberry Sauce.

12 6-INCH WAFFLES

2½ cups milk, warmed to about 115 degrees

2 teaspoons instant yeast, or 1 package very fresh active dry yeast

6 tablespoons unsalted butter, melted

1¼ teaspoons coarse salt

1 tablespoon granulated sugar

2 cups all-purpose flour, preferably bleached

2 eggs

¼ teaspoon baking soda

¾ teaspoon vanilla extract

Tarragon Strawberry Sauce (page 134)

Sweet Potato–Rosemary Waffles

Based on a distinctly Southern recipe, these waffles offer full flavor that's a nice change from the ordinary. If you have leftover cooked sweet potatoes, great; if not, canned ones work fine, if you drain them well. If you prefer, try using canned pumpkin instead. Serve these with butter and honey or maple syrup.

2 teaspoons minced rosemary leaves

2 cups all-purpose flour, preferably bleached

½ teaspoon coarse salt

1 tablespoon baking powder

3 eggs, separated

1½ cups mashed, cooked sweet potatoes

1½ cups milk

⅓ cup (packed) light brown sugar

4 tablespoons unsalted butter, melted

1. In a large bowl, whisk together rosemary leaves, flour, salt, and baking powder. In another bowl, whisk together egg yolks, sweet potatoes, milk, brown sugar, and butter. In a small bowl, beat or whisk egg whites until stiff peaks form.

2. Preheat a waffle iron according to manufacturer's instructions.

3. Pour sweet potato mixture over flour mixture; whisk until smooth (batter will be thick). With a rubber spatula, gently fold in beaten egg whites.

4. Ladle waffle batter onto the iron according to manufacturer's instructions, oiling iron first if needed. Cook until iron stops steaming; waffles should be crisp. Serve immediately.

10 6-INCH WAFFLES

Eierkuchen with Blackberry–Thyme Sauce

A specialty of both my mother and her mother, eierkuchen (say "eye-er-kook-en") is a thin German egg pancake akin to a crepe. Like strawberry shortcakes in the spring, eierkuchen was my family's splurge, forget-balanced-meals supper in wintertime. I suppose they make more sense for breakfast, but I like them any time of day. Blackberries were a traditional topping for us; we also passed sour cream and applesauce on the side.

1. In a large bowl, beat eggs until quite frothy, preferably with an electric mixer. Beat in flour, milk, and sugar on high speed (or by whisking briskly).

2. Heat a large skillet, preferably cast iron, over medium-high heat. Lightly grease the pan with just enough shortening to film it (even well-seasoned pans need greasing).

3. Pour in just enough batter to coat the skillet—from ¼ to ½ cup batter. Cook until bottom is crisp and golden, about 1½ to 2 minutes; flip with a wide spatula and cook 30 seconds to 1 minute more. Repeat with remaining batter; for each pancake, you must lightly grease the pan to achieve crisp, lacy edges.

4. Serve immediately with warm Blackberry–Thyme Sauce.

ABOUT 8 THIN 10-INCH PANCAKES

6 eggs

¾ cup all-purpose flour

1 ¾ cups plus 2 tablespoons milk

1 tablespoon granulated sugar

Vegetable shortening or canola oil as needed, for cooking

Blackberry–Thyme Sauce (page 135)

Raised Lemon Balm Pancakes

Like raised waffles, these pancakes have a delicate flavor, and they're wonderfully easy to prepare ahead. They're good with any fruit syrup, but especially tasty with the Lemon Thyme–Raspberry Syrup (page 136). Leftover batter may be stored in the refrigerator, tightly covered, for up to 2 days.

1 ¾ cups milk, warmed to about 115 degrees

2 teaspoons instant yeast, or 1 package very fresh active dry yeast

3 tablespoons unsalted butter, melted

1 teaspoon coarse salt, divided

2 tablespoons granulated sugar

2 cups all-purpose flour, preferably bleached

3 tablespoons minced lemon balm leaves

2 eggs

Canola oil as needed, for cooking

1. In a large bowl, whisk together milk, yeast, butter, ½ teaspoon salt, and the sugar, flour, and lemon balm leaves until very smooth. Cover bowl with plastic wrap and refrigerate overnight, or up to 3 days (batter may rise high). (If your kitchen is cool, leave the bowl on the counter overnight instead of chilling it.)

2. When you're ready to make pancakes, whisk eggs and remaining ½ teaspoon salt into batter (which may look separated); whisk until smooth. (At this point, batter may stand at room temperature up to 30 minutes.)

3. Heat a large skillet or griddle, preferably cast iron or nonstick, over medium-low heat. Very lightly film skillet with oil. Pour in as many pancakes as will fit, using about ¼ to ⅓ cup batter for each (batter will spread). Cook until bubbles appear around the edges and undersides are golden; flip pancakes and cook just until underside is golden. Serve immediately, with a warm sauce.

18 4-INCH PANCAKES

Apple–Savory German Puffed Pancake

Somewhat dramatic, this large pancake is fun to present at the table as soon as it comes out of the oven—expect the puff to fall quickly. If the handle of your pan isn't ovenproof, wrap it well with aluminum foil for protection.

1. Preheat oven to 425 degrees.

2. In a 10-inch skillet with an ovenproof handle (preferably cast iron), melt butter over medium-high heat. Add apples, winter savory leaves, and sugar. Cook, stirring frequently, until apples are slightly caramelized and tender but not mushy, about 3 minutes. Stir in lemon juice. Spread apples evenly over pan; remove from heat and set aside.

3. In a blender or food processor, thoroughly mix eggs, milk, flour, salt, and vanilla. Pour over apples; sprinkle with turbinado or brown sugar.

4. Bake pancake for 25 to 30 minutes, until puffed and golden. Serve immediately.

4 TO 6 SERVINGS

4 tablespoons unsalted butter

2 apples, peeled, cored, and thinly sliced

2½ teaspoons minced winter savory leaves

¼ cup granulated sugar

2 tablespoons fresh lemon juice

3 eggs

¾ cup milk

½ cup all-purpose flour

¼ teaspoon coarse salt

½ teaspoon vanilla extract

2 tablespoons turbinado sugar or (packed) light brown sugar

Cornmeal Crepes with Lemon Verbena–Ricotta Filling

I've always liked the flavor combination of cornmeal and lemon, delicate and fresh in these crepes. If you have a crepe pan, use it; the low, sloped sides are easy to work with. Otherwise, a small skillet works fine. You may have another way to flip crepes, but here's how I do it: Let the crepe cook until thoroughly set on top and golden underneath—the very fragile crepes will tear easily otherwise. Run a dull knife blade around the edge to loosen the crepe, then push the blade under the center of the crepe to release it, grasping the top with your thumb and/or a spatula, and flip the crepe. Expect to discard the first crepe or two until you get the technique and the heat right. See page xxxvi if you want to make the crepes ahead and freeze them before filling, but you can even cook and fill these crepes a day ahead, cover them in plastic, and then sauté them lightly in butter to warm them the next day.

CREPES

1 cup water

1 cup milk

3 eggs, at room
    temperature

½ cup cornmeal

½ cup all-purpose
    flour, preferably
    bleached

(Continued)

1. Make crepes: Place water, milk, eggs, cornmeal, flour, salt, sugar, and butter in a blender; blend until smooth. Let stand 30 minutes.

2. Meanwhile, make filling: Whisk together ricotta, lemon verbena leaves, cream, sugar, vanilla, and salt; stir in raisins if desired. Cover and chill until ready to use.

3. To cook crepes, heat a 6-inch crepe pan or other small skillet

over medium heat. Add just a touch of butter to coat the pan. Whisk crepe batter and pour about 2 tablespoons into skillet. Swirl the skillet to coat the bottom; if you have excess batter, pour it back into remaining crepe batter. Let cook until crepe is a deep golden on underside and set on top; then flip and cook until underside is flecked with brown. Remove to a plate. As you remove crepes, top each with a heaping tablespoon of filling placed just off-center. Fold crepe in half, then quarters, to make a triangle.

4. Repeat with remaining crepe batter, whisking it frequently and adding butter to pan as needed.

5. Serve crepes immediately as you fill them, dusting them with confectioners' sugar and topping with raspberries, if desired. Or, when all crepes are cooked and filled, lightly butter a large skillet set over medium heat and add as many folded crepes as fit in a single layer; let cook just until heated through. Sprinkle with confectioners' sugar and serve with berries.

20 6-INCH CREPES (4 TO 6 SERVINGS)

½ teaspoon coarse salt

3 tablespoons granulated sugar

3 tablespoons unsalted butter, melted

FILLING

1 ¼ cups ricotta cheese (preferably part-skim)

1 tablespoon minced lemon verbena leaves

¼ cup heavy cream

1 tablespoon granulated sugar

1 teaspoon vanilla extract

Pinch of coarse salt

⅓ cup golden raisins (optional)

Unsalted butter as needed, for cooking

GARNISH

Confectioners' sugar; raspberries (optional)

Cinnamon Basil French Toast

This French toast gets a delicate flavor from the cinnamon basil, which goes well with maple syrup. If you don't have a food processor, you can just whisk 2 tablespoons minced cinnamon basil leaves into the batter—but then it becomes even more important to dredge the bread to pick up some of the leaves. If you use sandwich bread, choose slices that are firm and dense—soft and spongy supermarket bread won't work. Based on French toast recipes I developed for *Cook's Illustrated* magazine (see also Nectarine-Stuffed French Toast, page 84), this batter creates French toast that is crisp outside and custardy inside. If you own a griddle that spans two burners, use it here if using sandwich bread.

¼ cup (packed) whole cinnamon basil leaves

3 tablespoons granulated sugar

1 egg

2 tablespoons unsalted butter, melted

¾ cup milk

1 teaspoon vanilla extract

⅓ cup all-purpose flour

½ teaspoon coarse salt

(Continued)

1. Place cinnamon basil leaves and sugar in a food processor; whiz until leaves are finely ground.

2. In a medium bowl, whisk together egg and butter. Whisk in milk and vanilla. Add flour, salt, cinnamon, and sugar mixture; whisk until smooth.

3. Heat a 10- to 12-inch skillet, preferably cast iron, over medium heat for about 3 minutes.

4. Transfer batter to a shallow pan or pie plate. Soak bread slices in batter (you may need to do this in 2 batches, depending on your skillet) for 30 seconds per side. Coat the hot skillet with ½ to 1

tablespoon butter. Remove bread from batter, pulling it through to pick up basil leaves, and add to skillet. Cook until golden, about 1 minute 45 seconds on the first side and 1 minute on the second side. Serve hot with syrup.

4 TO 6 SERVINGS

½ teaspoon ground cinnamon

4¾-inch slices challah (preferably day-old), or 6 to 8 slices firm sandwich bread

About 1 tablespoon unsalted butter, for frying

GARNISH

Warmed maple syrup

Nectarine-Stuffed French Toast

It's important to use day-old bread for this, as too-soft bread will stay soggy after cooking. Also, soak the bread in a shallow pan to keep too much batter from soaking in. This is tasty with a little maple syrup on the side. You may substitute a peach for the nectarine; I like the fuzzless skin of the nectarine better.

¼ cup (packed) whole basil leaves

3 tablespoons granulated sugar, divided

1 nectarine, diced

8 1-inch-thick slices day-old French or Italian bread

1 egg

1 cup milk

1½ teaspoons vanilla extract

1 tablespoon all-purpose flour

½ teaspoon coarse salt

About 2 tablespoons unsalted butter, for frying

GARNISH

Confectioners' sugar (optional); warmed maple syrup

4 TO 8 SERVINGS

1. Place basil leaves and 1 tablespoon sugar in a food processor; whiz until leaves are finely ground. Toss with nectarine; set aside.

2. Holding bread slices upright, cut each slice almost in half from top to bottom (leave the two halves connected at the bottom to form a pocket). Stuff these pockets with nectarine mixture and press gently to close.

3. In a medium bowl, whisk together egg, milk, vanilla, flour, salt, and remaining 2 tablespoons sugar. Pour into a shallow pan or pie plate.

4. Heat a 10- to 12-inch skillet, preferably cast iron, over medium heat for about 3 minutes.

5. Soak bread slices in batter (you may need to do this in 3 batches, depending on your skillet) for 20 seconds per side. Coat hot skillet with 1 tablespoon butter. Remove bread from batter and add to skillet. Cook until golden, about 1 minute 45 seconds on the first side and 1 minute on the second side. Dust with confectioners' sugar if desired; serve hot with syrup.

Cereals,

Cookies,

and

Puddings

Granola Three Ways

Vanilla yogurt with granola mixed in is one of my favorite breakfasts, but I hate spending the money on granola that is only OK—I usually find packaged granola too sweet, especially reduced-fat versions. I had a hard time coming up with a granola recipe that produced what I wanted: not lots of well-stirred, individual toasted flakes of oats, but crunchy, golden clusters of oats, almonds, and coconut. It turned out to be simple—just pack it down, and don't stir! You may use all honey instead of honey and corn syrup, but I find the texture slightly less crisp. Baking in the smaller pan and/or for the shorter baking time will also keep the cereal a little chewier, if you prefer that.

2 tablespoons
  unsalted butter

¼ cup light corn
  syrup

¼ cup honey

2¾ cups rolled oats

½ cup sliced almonds

½ cup (packed) light
  brown sugar

1½ teaspoons ground
  cinnamon

(Continued)

1. Preheat oven to 350 degrees. Butter an 11-by-15-inch jelly-roll pan, or a 9-by-13-inch baking pan.

2. In a small saucepan over medium heat, melt butter with corn syrup and honey until just liquefied.

3. Meanwhile, in a large bowl, stir together (or blend with a mixer on low speed) oats, almonds, brown sugar, cinnamon, and herb leaves. Mix in butter mixture until well combined.

4. Pack granola into buttered pan. Bake for 20 to 30 minutes, until dark golden. While granola is baking, in a small pan or on a piece of aluminum foil, bake coconut for about 5 to 7 minutes, until just golden.

5. Let granola cool for 5 minutes, then use a metal spatula or blunt knife to begin breaking it into bite-size chunks; it will seem soft and chewy but will crisp as it cools. Stir in coconut, and let cool completely in the pan. Store in an airtight container.

1 ¼ POUNDS

¼ cup minced cinnamon basil leaves, or 3 tablespoons minced allspice leaves, or 3 tablespoons minced tarragon leaves (if using tarragon, omit ground cinnamon)

½ cup flaked coconut (optional)

Granola Bars

I like these bars with the Basil or Allspice Granola variations, but feel free to experiment.

They're soft and chewy, with just a bit of granola crunch.

¾ cup dried cranberries

1¼ cups all-purpose flour

¾ teaspoon baking powder

½ teaspoon coarse salt

2¼ cups Granola (page 88)

1 cup (packed) light brown sugar

6 tablespoons unsalted butter, melted

3 egg whites

1. Preheat oven to 350 degrees. Grease a 9-by-13-inch baking pan.

2. In a medium bowl, whisk together cranberries, flour, baking powder, salt, and granola. In a small bowl, whisk together brown sugar, butter, and egg whites. Pour over flour mixture and fold in thoroughly with a rubber spatula. Spread in prepared pan.

3. Bake bars for 25 to 30 minutes, until golden and top is set. Let cool on a wire rack before cutting.

16 BARS

Fruited Lemon Biscotti

I'm a big fan of biscotti, and they make a nice addition to a breakfast tray or a brunch. I'm also a big fan of candied fruit (this stems from my love of my mother's stollen, a German Christmas bread). I use the dreaded "fruit cake mix" and think it tastes just right. If this isn't quite to your taste, you could use chopped dried fruit instead (which may be easier to find in summer; I keep a container of the fruit cake mix in the freezer for summer cravings).

1. Preheat oven to 350 degrees.

2. In a food processor, whiz together lemon verbena leaves and sugar until leaves are ground. Transfer to a medium bowl and whisk in eggs and vanilla until blended. In another bowl, whisk together flour, baking powder, and salt; stir in candied fruit. Fold into egg mixture with a rubber spatula until incorporated. Dough will be sticky.

3. Divide dough in half. Wet your hands and shake them off, but don't dry them. On a parchment paper–lined baking sheet, press each half into a log that measures 11 inches long by 2 inches wide; press down on top until it's ½ inch high. Leave about 2 inches between logs.

4. Bake for 30 to 35 minutes, until golden. Remove from oven; lower heat to 325 degrees. Cool pans on a wire rack for 15 minutes. Transfer logs to a cutting board and cut crosswise with a serrated knife into ¾-inch slices. Return slices, standing up, to the parchment-lined baking sheet, spaced slightly apart. Bake 15 minutes more, until crisp. Transfer to wire racks to cool.

¼ cup whole lemon verbena leaves

1 cup granulated sugar

2 eggs

1 teaspoon vanilla extract

1¾ cups all-purpose flour

1 teaspoon baking powder

½ teaspoon coarse salt

1 cup chopped candied fruit

2½ DOZEN BISCOTTI

Apple–Anise Oatmeal Cookies

I'm fond of the flavor of anise hyssop in small doses; in these cookies it's a nice background flavor, making the cookies a bit more complex. These cookies are soft and chewy; bake them a little longer if you like crisp cookies. They're great as an ending to a simple brunch, or when you're hungry and in a hurry.

⅔ cup granulated sugar

⅔ cup (packed) light brown sugar

½ cup plus 2 tablespoons (1¼ sticks) unsalted butter, softened

2 teaspoons vanilla extract

2 eggs

1⅔ cups all-purpose flour

2 tablespoons minced anise hyssop leaves

1 teaspoon baking soda

¾ teaspoon coarse salt

2 cups rolled oats

1 medium tart apple, peeled and diced

1. Preheat oven to 325 degrees.

2. In a large bowl, beat granulated sugar, brown sugar, and butter on high speed until light and fluffy. Beat in vanilla. Beat in eggs 1 at a time, beating well after each addition. Add flour, anise hyssop leaves, baking soda, and salt; beat on low speed until combined. Beat in oats and apples until just combined.

3. Drop scant tablespoonsful of dough on parchment paper–lined or lightly greased baking sheets, about 2 inches apart. Bake for 20 to 22 minutes, until golden brown. Cool pans on wire racks; cookies should be almost completely cooled before removing. Store in an airtight container, separating the layers with waxed paper.

4 DOZEN COOKIES

Banana–Basil Oatmeal Sandwich Cookies

These are hearty, filling cookies, perfect for a hectic morning. I love the extra flavor of the peanut butter filling, but the cookies also taste great without it.

1. Preheat oven to 325 degrees.

2. In a large bowl, beat granulated sugar, brown sugar, and butter on high speed until light and fluffy. Beat in vanilla. Beat in eggs 1 at a time, beating well after each. Beat in banana just until combined; mixture will appear curdled. Add flour, cinnamon basil or regular basil leaves, baking soda, salt, and cinnamon; beat on low speed until combined. Beat in oats until just combined.

3. Drop scant tablespoonsful of dough on parchment paper–lined or lightly greased baking sheets, about 2 inches apart. Bake for 14 to 16 minutes, until golden brown. Cool pans on wire racks; cookies should be almost completely cooled before removing.

4. If necessary, beat peanut butter in a small bowl until smooth and spreadable. Spread the flat bottoms of half the cookies with the peanut butter; top with remaining cookies, flat side facing the filling. Store in an airtight container, separating the layers with waxed paper.

2 DOZEN SANDWICH COOKIES

⅔ cup granulated sugar

⅔ cup (packed) light brown sugar

½ cup (1 stick) unsalted butter, softened

1 teaspoon vanilla extract

2 eggs

1 cup mashed ripe bananas

2⅓ cups all-purpose flour

⅓ cup minced cinnamon basil or regular basil leaves

1 teaspoon baking soda

¾ teaspoon coarse salt

½ teaspoon ground cinnamon

2 cups rolled oats

1 cup peanut butter (smooth or crunchy; reduced-fat is fine)

Pecan–Banana Bread Pudding

Bread pudding for breakfast? Sure, especially when it's light, moist, and not too sweet. Don't use skim milk here; it makes the pudding too watery, although 2 percent milk works well. Of course, you can always go richer, with whole milk or some half-and-half or cream. To make this ahead, simply prepare it at night without cooking it, cover it, and put it in the refrigerator; the next morning, place it in a cold oven (uncovered), turn the oven to 350 degrees, and bake, adding 5 to 10 minutes extra, or as needed.

1 loaf (about 12 ounces) French bread or good-quality sandwich bread, cut into ½-inch cubes (about 5 packed cups)

2 or 3 medium, firm-ripe bananas

½ cup chopped pecans

3 cups milk

4 eggs

1 ¼ cups granulated sugar

1 teaspoon vanilla extract

1 ½ teaspoons minced allspice leaves

½ teaspoon coarse salt

6 SERVINGS

1. Preheat oven to 350 degrees. Lightly grease or butter a 2- or 2½-quart baking dish (I use an oval one); place half the bread cubes in the dish.

2. Thinly slice the bananas and distribute them over the bread; sprinkle with pecans. Top with remaining bread cubes.

3. Heat milk in a small saucepan just until steaming. In a medium bowl, whisk together eggs, sugar, vanilla, allspice leaves, and salt. Very slowly whisk in hot milk. Pour over the bread mixture. Briefly press down on bread cubes so they absorb some of the liquid.

4. Fill a pitcher with very hot tap water. Place the baking dish in a 9-by-13-inch pan; place pan in the oven. Pour hot water into the pan to come halfway up the sides of the baking dish.

5. Bake for 60 minutes, or until puffed and just set; top will be crusty. Serve hot.

Chocolate, Cranberry, and Lavender Bread Pudding

OK, so the previous recipe says I like light bread puddings for breakfast. This is a significantly richer brunch dish, but so good on a cold winter's day. My first test of this recipe came out of the oven just as I was preparing a healthful pregnancy lunch of a tuna sandwich. Of course, I had to test it while it was hot. Two servings later, I felt vaguely guilty about missing that sandwich—but the baby didn't seem to mind.

1. Preheat oven to 350 degrees. Lightly grease or butter a 2- or 2½-quart baking dish (I use an oval one).

2. Heat milk in a small saucepan just until steaming. In a large bowl, whisk together eggs, sugar, salt, and vanilla. Very slowly whisk in hot milk. Fold in bread cubes; pour mixture into the prepared baking dish.

3. Fill a small pitcher with hot water. Put baking dish into a 9-by-13-inch pan and place in the oven; pour in hot water to come one-third of the way up the sides of the baking dish.

4. Bake for 60 minutes, or until pudding is just set and top is crusty. Serve hot.

6 SERVINGS

3 cups milk (low-fat or whole, not skim)

4 eggs

1¼ cups granulated sugar

½ teaspoon coarse salt

1 teaspoon vanilla extract

½ loaf Chocolate, Cranberry, and Lavender Bread (page 60), cut into ½-inch cubes (about 5 cups)

Bay Rice Pudding with Granola Crunch

I am a huge rice pudding fan, at least when it's done right—creamy and rich. This makes a perfect breakfast for a cold day, especially with the contrasting crunch of granola. Although it's best right from the oven, it also reheats nicely in the microwave; just be sure to hold the initial baking to no more than 65 minutes total. That way the pudding will stay creamy in the reheating, even if it looks a tad sloshy at first.

1 ½ cups heavy cream

1 ½ cups milk

1 tablespoon unsalted butter

½ cup Arborio or medium-grain rice

¼ cup granulated sugar

½ teaspoon coarse salt

1 large fresh bay leaf or 2 medium leaves

1 ½ teaspoons vanilla extract

About 1 ½ cups Granola (page 86), preferably allspice variation

1. Preheat oven to 325 degrees. Butter a 2-quart or larger baking dish.

2. Whisk together cream, milk, butter (not melted—it will melt in baking), rice, sugar, and salt. Pour into baking dish.

3. Cover and bake for 30 minutes. Whisk briefly and submerge bay leaf in the mixture. Cover and bake for 35 to 40 minutes more. The pudding should be slightly saucy and the rice barely chewy; it will thicken upon standing.

4. Remove bay leaf; stir in vanilla, and let stand 5 minutes before serving.

5. To serve, divide the pudding among 4 or 6 serving bowls; sprinkle each with about ¼ cup Granola.

4 TO 6 SERVINGS

Cinnamon Basil Sweet Grits Brûlée

I can't say I'd make these every day, but they're wonderful for brunch—unexpected, and they feel decadent (though they're actually low-fat when made with skim milk). Serve hot, but look out—it's easy to burn your mouth. These may be made ahead to the point of filling the ramekins and chilling them. Reheat in a microwave or 350-degree oven before caramelizing the tops.

1. Lightly grease 6 6-ounce ramekins (measuring about 3 inches across) and place them on a baking sheet. Rinse a small saucepan with cold water; shake out but do not dry (this helps keep the milk from sticking and burning). Pour milk into pan and bring to a boil.

2. Put grits in a medium saucepan; slowly pour in boiling milk, whisking constantly. Bring to a boil, whisking, over medium-high heat. Reduce heat to low, cover, and simmer 5 minutes, whisking twice.

3. Remove grits from heat; whisk in brown sugar, cinnamon basil leaves, cinnamon, vanilla, and butter. Divide among ramekins; sprinkle each with 1 ½ teaspoons turbinado sugar.

4. Preheat broiler. Run ramekins under broiler, turning baking sheet as needed, until turbinado sugar caramelizes (watch that it doesn't burn badly). (Alternatively, use a blowtorch to caramelize the sugar—this gives you more control and works faster.) Serve immediately.

6 SERVINGS

---

3 ¾ cups milk

¾ cup quick-cooking grits (not instant)

¼ cup packed light or dark brown sugar

3 tablespoons minced cinnamon basil leaves

1 teaspoon ground cinnamon

1 teaspoon vanilla extract

1 tablespoon unsalted butter

3 tablespoons turbinado sugar (or use light brown sugar)

Fruit

Dishes

Lavender Sautéed Apples

Lavender really perks up plain cooked apples. If you like, take the cooking of these a little further, until quite soft, and mash them into applesauce. I like the stronger flavor of dark brown sugar in this, but either light or dark works well.

1 tablespoon unsalted butter

1 ½ teaspoons dried lavender

4 medium, tart apples, peeled, each cut into 16 slices

½ cup (packed) brown sugar

1 tablespoon fresh lemon juice, or more to taste

1. In a large skillet over medium heat, melt butter. Crush lavender lightly with your fingers and add to butter; stir in apples. Cook, stirring often, until apples begin to soften, about 3 to 5 minutes.

2. Stir in brown sugar; continue cooking for 3 to 5 minutes more, until apples are softened and syrupy. Remove from heat and stir in 1 tablespoon lemon juice (add more if apples seem too sweet). Serve hot. Apples may be made ahead and reheated over low heat.

4 TO 6 SERVINGS

Sage Honey–Glazed Sautéed Pears

These incredibly simple pears make a pretty presentation on a plate; depending on what else is served, you may count a half or a whole pear as one serving. I prefer to make this with Bosc pears.

1. Halve pears lengthwise; scoop out seeds and blossom end with a melon baller or spoon (I leave the stem intact when possible).

2. In a large skillet over medium heat, melt butter. Add pears, flat side down, and let cook until slightly softened and golden, about 4 minutes. Carefully turn pears over and continue cooking until softened and golden, about 3 more minutes. Pour sage honey over and around pears. Continue cooking, turning pears once more, until honey bubbles and liquefies and glazes pears.

3. To serve, transfer pears to serving plates and drizzle with glaze from pan. Serve hot or warm.

4 TO 8 SERVINGS

4 firm-ripe pears, peeled

1 tablespoon unsalted butter

¼ cup Sage Honey (page 137)

Baked Pineapple with Basil

Especially since many supermarkets now carry peeled and cored whole pineapples, this three-ingredient recipe is about as easy as can be, but luscious. I like any leftovers cut up and stirred into yogurt or cottage cheese. If you can't find turbinado sugar but can find granulated brown sugar, use it—it sprinkles easily.

1 pineapple, peeled, cored, and cut into ½-inch-thick rings

3 tablespoons turbinado sugar or light brown sugar

1 tablespoon minced basil leaves

1. Preheat oven to 350 degrees.

2. Place pineapple rings on a baking sheet, preferably one lined with parchment paper. Sprinkle rings with sugar. Bake for 20 minutes, until sugar has melted and pineapple is heated through.

3. Sprinkle rings with basil leaves and serve immediately.

4 TO 6 SERVINGS

Rhubarb, Blueberry, and Orange Compote

This compote may be served warm or chilled; either way it's simply fabulous. If you can't find good fresh blueberries at the same time as rhubarb, thawed frozen berries will work fine, or try strawberries instead, a classic combination. Rhubarb goes to mush in seconds, so be diligent about testing often after 6 minutes of cooking. Be sure to use only the rhubarb stalks, not the leaves. Should you have leftovers, they're a great topping for angel food cake or frozen yogurt. Great alone, this compote can also be dressed up with a drizzle of vanilla yogurt or heavy cream.

1. In a large saucepan, stir together orange zest, juice, and sugar. Bring to a boil over high heat; boil 1 minute.

2. Add angelica leaves and rhubarb; reduce heat to medium or medium-low and cook at a bare simmer for 6 to 10 minutes, until rhubarb is just tender. After 6 minutes of cooking, test rhubarb about every 30 seconds so it doesn't overcook. Remove from heat and let cool 5 minutes.

3. Meanwhile, peel and pull apart segments of remaining orange; cut each segment in half crosswise. Stir into compote with blueberries. Serve immediately or chill.

3 ¾ CUPS

Grated zest of 2 oranges

Juice of 2 oranges plus water as needed to equal 1 cup

1 ¼ cups granulated sugar

1 tablespoon minced angelica leaves

1 pound rhubarb stalks, cut into ½-inch slices

1 whole orange

2 cups (1 pint) blueberries

Layered Fruit Salad

Use this recipe just as a guideline, especially for quantities; you could easily substitute or add

honeydew melon, pineapple, other berries, pears, apples, cherries, grapes—you get the idea.

Or try another herb, such as pineapple mint, lemon or lime basil, or lemon verbena. My main

requirement in making this salad is to use a shallow glass bowl so the layers show. I also try to

avoid color clashes, such as red strawberries on top of orange cantaloupe. You may mince the

herb leaves if you prefer; just don't leave them whole (especially if they're large), as their fuzzy

texture would overwhelm the fruit. Serve this salad plain, or with a bowl of vanilla yogurt or

sweetened, pureed cottage cheese on the side (see page 72).

2 large or 3 medium
   oranges

4 kiwis

1 pound strawberries

½ large cantaloupe

1 large banana

About 20 medium
   pineapple sage or
   citrus sage leaves

1. With a sharp knife, cut a small slice off the top and bottom of each orange. Remove peel by slicing from top to bottom, removing all the white pith. Turn oranges on their sides and slice into thin rounds. Set aside.

2. Cut a small slice off the top and bottom of each kiwi. Insert a spoon gently just under the peel (with the inside of the bowl of the spoon facing kiwi flesh), then rotate kiwi to dislodge peel. Slice each kiwi into thin rounds. Set aside.

3. Stem and halve strawberries. With a melon baller, scoop out cantaloupe balls (alternatively, cut cantaloupe flesh into small cubes). Cut banana into thin rounds.

4. Set aside 4 pineapple sage or citrus sage leaves. With a sharp knife or kitchen shears, cut remaining leaves into thin strips.

5. Place a single layer of kiwi slices in a medium glass serving bowl. Continue layering fruit in this order: orange rounds, banana slices, cantaloupe balls, kiwi slices, herb leaves, strawberries; repeat, beginning with kiwi slices and ending with strawberries. Garnish with reserved whole herb leaves. Serve immediately or chill up to 8 hours.

6 SERVINGS

Allspice Applesauce

A chunky homemade applesauce tastes so much better than the overly runny versions from the supermarket, and when it's this quick, it's hard to find reasons to buy applesauce again. I own a lot of gadgets that don't get used much, but my apple slicer (a round tool with handles that simultaneously cores and slices an apple with a downward shove) has proved suprisingly useful over the past several years. I prefer fairly tart apples here; try Arkansas Black, Braeburn, or Rome apples.

4 large apples, each peeled, cored, and cut into 6 to 8 slices

2 tablespoons minced allspice leaves

½ cup water

⅓ cup (packed) light brown sugar

2 tablespoons fresh lemon juice, or more as needed

1. In a skillet over medium-high heat, stir together apples, allspice leaves, and water. Bring to a boil; cook, stirring often, for 10 minutes.

2. Stir in brown sugar and lemon juice; continue cooking and stirring for about 5 minutes, until apples are mushy. In the skillet, smash apples with a wooden spoon, pastry blender, potato masher, or fork. Taste and add a little more lemon juice if needed. Serve warm, or transfer to an airtight container and chill up to 1 week.

2 ¾ CUPS

Savory

Starts

Basil–Blue Cheese Frittata

Easy, pretty, delicious, open to variations—these are my kind of eggs. Frittatas are simply open-faced omelets that get finished in the oven, giving you a few minutes to set the table, or slice some bread, or simply drink a cup of tea. If you like, you can cut out 2 eggs here, or substitute 2 egg whites for 1 egg (for best flavor, substitute for no more than 3 whole eggs). You can also leave out the corn; or add fresh diced tomatoes, julienned spinach leaves, or sliced mushrooms (cook the mushrooms at the beginning, like the corn; add the others when you add the cheese). I like frittatas best hot from the oven, but they are also good at room temperature.

1 tablespoon unsalted butter

1 cup cooked corn kernels (or frozen corn, defrosted)

8 eggs

2 tablespoons milk or light cream

Pinch of coarse salt

Freshly ground black pepper to taste

¼ cup julienned basil leaves

¼ pound blue cheese, crumbled

GARNISH

Whole basil leaves

1. Preheat oven to 400 degrees. In a large skillet, preferably cast iron or enameled cast iron with an ovenproof handle (or cover handle well with foil), melt butter over medium heat. Add corn and cook, stirring, about 2 minutes.

2. In a medium bowl, whisk together eggs, milk, salt, and pepper until well combined. Pour into skillet. Let mixture just begin to set, then stir with a spatula, beginning from the middle and working out, to get uncooked egg onto bottom of skillet. Keep lifting cooked edges of egg to allow uncooked egg to run underneath.

3. When eggs are about halfway set, sprinkle basil leaves and blue cheese over top. Transfer skillet to the oven.

4. Bake frittata for 7 to 10 minutes, until eggs are just set. Remove

from oven, cut into wedges, and serve, garnishing with basil leaves. Or if you prefer, you may loosen the edges of the frittata with a knife and slide the whole frittata onto a serving platter.

4 TO 6 SERVINGS

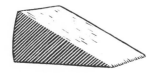

Thyme and Goat Cheese Frittata

Rich with fragrant goat cheese, this makes a quick breakfast or brunch dish. As with the basil frittata, you may substitute 2 egg whites for 1 egg (for best flavor, substitute for no more than 3 whole eggs). Feel free to experiment, adding other ingredients to this dish—though I like my goat cheese pure and strong. I do like a side dish of Grilled Tomatoes (page 121) with this.

2 tablespoons minced thyme leaves

8 eggs

2 tablespoons milk or light cream

Pinch of coarse salt

Freshly ground black pepper to taste

1 tablespoon unsalted butter

4 ounces goat cheese, crumbled

GARNISH

Minced thyme leaves or whole thyme sprigs

1. Preheat oven to 400 degrees.

2. In a medium bowl, whisk together thyme leaves, eggs, milk, salt, and pepper until well combined.

3. In a large skillet, preferably cast iron or enameled cast iron with an ovenproof handle (or cover handle well with foil), melt butter over medium heat. Pour egg mixture into skillet. Let mixture just begin to set, then stir with a spatula, beginning from the middle and working out, to get uncooked egg onto bottom of skillet. Keep lifting cooked edges of egg to allow uncooked egg to run underneath.

4. When eggs are about halfway set, sprinkle goat cheese over top. Transfer skillet to the oven.

5. Bake frittata for 7 to 10 minutes, until eggs are just set. Remove from oven, cut into wedges, and serve, garnishing wedges or the plate with thyme. Or if you prefer, you may loosen the edges of the frittata with a knife and slide the whole frittata onto a serving platter.

4 TO 6 SERVINGS

Sage, Smoked Cheddar, and Apple Omelet

Folded omelets are easy to make and so tasty, it's a wonder we tend to eat them only at restaurants. This is an especially great combination of flavors, sweet and smoky and just right for a chilly fall morning. If you can't find smoked cheddar, substitute a sharp cheddar. To make more than one serving at a time, double the recipe and cook it in a large skillet (my preference), or make each omelet separately and hold them briefly in a warm oven until you're ready to serve. As with frittatas, you may substitute 2 egg whites for 1 of the eggs.

1. In a medium bowl, whisk eggs, milk, salt, and pepper just until combined. In a 6- to 8-inch skillet (preferably nonstick), melt butter over medium-high heat.

2. Pour in egg mixture. As egg sets around the edges, lift edges and allow uncooked egg to run underneath, tilting pan as necessary. When top is almost set, sprinkle half the omelet with sage leaves, apple, and cheese. Allow to cook about 30 seconds more; fold uncovered half of omelet over filling and slide omelet onto a plate. Serve immediately, garnished on the side with apple slices and cheese if desired.

1 SERVING

3 eggs

1 tablespoon milk

Large pinch of coarse salt

Large pinch of freshly ground black pepper

1 teaspoon unsalted butter

½ teaspoon minced sage leaves

2 tablespoons diced, unpeeled apple

2 tablespoons grated smoked cheddar cheese

GARNISH

Thin slices of apple and a slice of smoked cheddar cheese (optional)

Herbed Mushroom Omelet

Here's how to make omelets that serve more than 1 person. The mushrooms would blend well with many other herbs: Try sage in place of the rosemary and thyme in place of the chives; or 1 tablespoon savory leaves or dill leaves; or 2 teaspoons parsley, 1 teaspoon thyme, and 1 teaspoon marjoram leaves. For the mushrooms, I like to use a blend of wild, button, and creminis, but feel free to experiment here, too. If you can find them, pre-sliced wild mushrooms speed things up; note that some wild mushrooms need their tough stems removed.

2 teaspoons unsalted butter, divided

6 ounces mixed mushrooms, thinly sliced

1 ½ teaspoons minced rosemary leaves

6 eggs

2 tablespoons milk

Large pinch of coarse salt

Large pinch of freshly ground black pepper

2 teaspoons minced chives

GARNISH

Sour cream and minced chives (optional)

1. In a 10-inch skillet (preferably nonstick or cast iron), melt 1 teaspoon butter over medium-high heat. Add mushrooms and rosemary leaves; cook, stirring often, until mushrooms are softened and browned, about 4 minutes. Transfer to a bowl with a slotted spoon.

2. In a medium bowl, whisk eggs, milk, salt, and pepper together just until combined. Melt remaining 1 teaspoon butter in skillet. Pour in egg mixture. As egg sets around the edges, lift edges and allow uncooked egg to run underneath, tilting pan as necessary. When top is almost set, sprinkle half the omelet with mushroom mixture and chives. Allow to cook about 30 seconds more; fold uncovered half of omelet over filling and slide omelet onto a plate. Divide into serving portions and serve immediately, garnishing with a dollop of sour cream and chives if desired.

2 TO 3 SERVINGS

Bacon, Brie, and Basil Omelet

Rummaging around the fridge one night for dinner, I created a bacon, brie, and basil pasta dish with tomatoes; it was great, but my husband and I like the combination even better in this omelet. Serve Grilled Tomatoes (page 121) on the side. If you prefer, divide the recipe in half to make individual omelets in a 6- to 8-inch pan.

1. In a medium bowl, whisk eggs, milk, salt, and pepper just until combined. In a 10-inch skillet (preferably nonstick or cast iron), melt butter over medium-high heat. Pour in egg mixture.

2. As egg sets around the edges, lift edges and allow uncooked egg to run underneath, tilting pan as necessary. When top is almost set, sprinkle half the omelet with bacon, brie, and basil leaves. Let cook about 30 seconds more; fold uncovered half of omelet over filling and slide omelet onto a plate. Divide into serving portions and serve immediately, garnishing with basil leaves if desired.

2 TO 3 SERVINGS

6 eggs

2 tablespoons milk

Large pinch of coarse salt

Large pinch of freshly ground black pepper

2 teaspoons unsalted butter

4 strips bacon, cooked and crumbled

¼ cup (about 1 ½ ounces) diced brie

¼ cup julienned basil leaves

GARNISH

Julienned basil leaves (optional)

Scrambled Egg Wrap with Cilantro, Tomatoes, and Feta

So long as you're a neat eater, these are a good breakfast on-the-go, full of flavor and easy to prepare. Make it even easier by mincing the cilantro and lemon verbena leaves, dicing the tomatoes, and crumbling the feta the night before. A hint: Unless you've found a brand you can trust, don't use fat-free tortillas, especially whole wheat ones—I find that they break and tear too easily. If you prefer, substitute 2 egg whites per whole egg (preferably substituting for no more than 4 of the whole eggs) to reduce the fat content.

8 eggs

¼ cup water

2 tablespoons minced cilantro leaves

½ teaspoon coarse salt

Freshly ground black pepper to taste

1 tablespoon unsalted butter

2 plum tomatoes, diced

½ cup crumbled feta cheese

1 teaspoon minced lemon verbena leaves (or use the grated zest of a small lemon)

4 7-inch flour tortillas, warmed according to package directions

1. In a medium bowl, whisk together eggs, water, cilantro leaves, salt, and pepper. Place a large skillet or sauté pan over medium heat; add butter. When butter just begins to bubble, pour in eggs.

2. As eggs begin to set, keep pushing them to one side to let the remaining eggs set. When the eggs are almost done, stir in tomatoes, feta, and lemon verbena leaves; keep stirring until mixture is heated through and cheese has melted slightly. Remove from heat.

3. Divide eggs among tortillas, placing eggs in a line down the center of each tortilla. Fold up bottom of tortilla, then fold in sides. Serve immediately.

4 SERVINGS

Quick Quiche

This quiche, filled with the classic herbs of Provence, is missing a crust but has a little more body than a simple egg custard. I like the extra flavor added by the buttermilk, but you could use all regular milk instead, or use buttermilk powder if you keep it on hand.

1. Preheat oven to 350 degrees. Grease a 9- or 10-inch pie plate or quiche dish.

2. In a large skillet, melt butter over medium heat. Pour all but about 1 tablespoon of the butter into a medium bowl. Add onion and mushrooms to skillet; cook, stirring, until vegetables are softened. With a slotted spoon, transfer vegetables to prepared pie plate, leaving behind any liquid remaining in skillet.

3. Add eggs, milk, and buttermilk to bowl of butter; whisk thoroughly. Add flour, baking powder, baking soda, salt, pepper, marjoram leaves, oregano leaves, thyme leaves, and savory leaves; whisk thoroughly (some lumps may remain). Pour into pie plate. Sprinkle evenly with cheese.

4. Bake quiche for 35 to 45 minutes, until top is browned and quiche is set in the middle. Let stand 5 to 10 minutes before serving. (If not serving immediately, cover and chill; reheat in a 350-degree oven for 15 minutes or as needed.)

6 TO 8 SERVINGS

---

6 tablespoons unsalted butter

1 onion, minced

¾ pound mushrooms, thinly sliced

3 eggs

1 cup milk

½ cup buttermilk

⅓ cup all-purpose flour

½ teaspoon baking powder

½ teaspoon baking soda

¾ teaspoon coarse salt

½ teaspoon freshly ground black pepper

1 teaspoon minced marjoram leaves

1 teaspoon minced oregano leaves

1 ¾ teaspoons minced thyme leaves

1 teaspoon minced savory leaves

1 cup shredded Swiss cheese

Roasted Vegetable Galette

Fragrant with oregano and thyme, this is a simple, rustic tart with a crust that I love. Lower in fat than standard pastry crusts, this crust takes very little work and tastes terrific. If you prefer, though, you may substitute your favorite pie or tart crust. You should also feel free to substitute other vegetables for the filling; this is simply one of my favorite combinations. Finally, you may roast or sauté the mushrooms if you prefer; I like mine raw. (To roast the mushrooms, just toss with a little olive oil and add to the zucchini and onions.) If you don't serve the galette immediately, reheat it thoroughly in a 350-degree oven to re-crisp the crust.

½ cup warm water

1 egg, lightly beaten

4 tablespoons extra-virgin olive oil, divided

About 2 cups unbleached all-purpose flour, divided

½ teaspoon coarse salt plus more to taste

1 ¼ teaspoons instant yeast, or 1 envelope very fresh active dry yeast

1 medium eggplant

2 small zucchini

1 medium yellow onion

(Continued)

1. In a medium bowl, whisk together water, egg, and 3 tablespoons olive oil. Stir in 1 ¾ cups flour, ½ teaspoon salt, and yeast. Add enough remaining flour to make a soft dough. Turn onto a floured board; knead until smooth and elastic, about 4 minutes (or knead with a heavy-duty mixer's dough hook for 90 seconds on medium speed). Place in a clean bowl; cover directly with a piece of greased plastic wrap, and set aside to rise for about 1 hour.

2. Meanwhile, preheat oven to 425 degrees. Peel the eggplant and slice into ¼-inch rounds. Slice zucchini into thin rounds. Peel onion and slice into thin rounds. Place eggplant on one parchment paper–lined or lightly greased baking sheet and zucchini and onion on another; brush all lightly with remaining 1 tablespoon olive oil. Bake eggplant slices for 30 minutes; remove zucchini and onion after 20 minutes, or when lightly browned. Leave oven on.

3. When dough is ready, roll it out on a lightly floured board into a 14-inch circle (a rough circle is fine). Transfer to a parchment paper–lined or lightly greased baking sheet. Top with eggplant slices, leaving a ½-inch border around the edge. Sprinkle eggplant with oregano leaves. Top with onion slices, then zucchini, then mushrooms. Sprinkle with thyme leaves. Top with tomato slices; sprinkle tomatoes with salt and pepper to taste. Top with cheese slices.

4. Fold dough border up over the edge of the tart, pleating it to make an attractive rim. Bake galette for 25 to 30 minutes, until crust is golden and crisp. Serve immediately.

6 TO 8 SERVINGS

1½ tablespoons minced oregano leaves

4 ounces mushrooms (wild or button, or a mixture), thinly sliced

1 tablespoon minced thyme leaves

2 large tomatoes, thinly sliced

Freshly ground black pepper to taste

5 slices (about ¼ pound) Provolone cheese

Havarti–Dill Grits

I'm a Southerner by birth but not by heritage—but you'd never know it from my love of grits.

Even my husband, who can't stand them plain, adores cheese grits. They're commonly made

with cheddar cheese, but this version gives a more delicate flavor that's perfect in the morning—

interesting but not jarring. Look for grits that say they take 5 minutes to cook, not instant grits.

You can use the lower amount of cheese and cut the butter in half if you prefer, but the rich flavor

of these is worth a splurge. The grits reheat well, so feel free to bake them the night before.

4 cups water

1 cup quick-cooking grits (see headnote)

½ teaspoon coarse salt

Freshly ground black pepper to taste (at least ¼ teaspoon)

4 to 6 ounces Havarti cheese, diced

1 tablespoon plus 2 teaspoons minced dill leaves, divided

4 tablespoons unsalted butter

2 eggs, lightly beaten

1. Preheat oven to 350 degrees; lightly grease a 2 to 2½-quart baking dish. Bring water to a boil in a small saucepan.

2. Put grits in a large saucepan; slowly pour in boiling water, whisking constantly. Bring to a boil, whisking, over medium-high heat. Stir in salt and pepper; reduce heat, cover, and simmer 5 minutes, whisking twice.

3. Remove grits from heat; stir in cheese, 1 tablespoon dill leaves, and butter until melted. Whisk a little of grits mixture into the beaten eggs to warm them; slowly pour egg mixture into grits, whisking constantly. Pour into prepared baking dish.

4. Bake grits, uncovered, for 45 to 50 minutes or until just set. Let stand 10 minutes before serving; sprinkle with remaining 2 teaspoons dill leaves to serve. (If not serving immediately, cover and chill. Reheat in a microwave or 325-degree oven.)

6 TO 8 SERVINGS

Smoked Cheddar and Chive Grits

Molding the grits in ramekins makes a more special presentation, and it's easy, but you can always use a 2-quart baking dish instead. These may be made the night before and reheated.

1. Preheat oven to 350 degrees; lightly grease 6 to 8 6-ounce ramekins (measuring about 3 inches across) and place them on a baking sheet. Bring water to a boil in a small saucepan.

2. Put grits in a medium saucepan; pour in boiling water, whisking constantly. Bring to a boil, whisking, over medium-high heat. Stir in salt and pepper; reduce heat, cover, and simmer 5 minutes, whisking twice.

3. Remove grits from heat; stir in cheese, 3 tablespoons chives, and butter until melted. Whisk a little of grits mixture into the beaten eggs to warm them; slowly pour egg mixture into grits, whisking constantly. Divide among ramekins.

4. Bake grits, uncovered, for 30 to 35 minutes or until just set. Let stand 10 minutes before serving. Serve in the ramekins, sprinkled with remaining 2 teaspoons chives. Or if you prefer, run a knife around the edges of each ramekin and invert onto serving plates, then sprinkle with chives. (If not serving immediately, cover and chill. Reheat in a microwave or 325-degree oven.)

6 TO 8 SERVINGS

4 cups water

1 cup quick-cooking grits (see headnote on previous recipe)

½ teaspoon coarse salt

Freshly ground black pepper to taste (at least ¼ teaspoon)

4 ounces smoked cheddar cheese, diced

3 tablespoons plus 2 teaspoons minced chives, divided

3 tablespoons unsalted butter

2 eggs, lightly beaten

Cilantro Turkey Sausage

I love sausage, but not all the fat it usually contains. This is a good compromise, with lots of flavor but much less fat than pork sausage. If you can, buy ½ pound each of ground turkey breast and ground turkey thighs, for the best combination of flavor and reduced fat.

1 medium yellow onion, peeled and halved

3 cloves garlic, peeled

⅓ cup minced cilantro

1 pound ground turkey

1 teaspoon coarse salt

1 teaspoon paprika

1 teaspoon freshly ground black pepper

1 tablespoon canola or olive oil, or more as needed

1. Finely mince onion and garlic by hand or in a food processor. Stir in cilantro, turkey, salt, paprika, and pepper; mix gently but thoroughly with a rubber spatula.

2. If you want to make patties, form mixture into 15 3-inch circles.

3. Heat the oil in a large skillet over medium heat. For patties, cook on each side about 3 to 4 minutes, until golden and cooked through; for bulk sausage, simply cook, stirring often, until cooked through and no longer pink.

4. Serve hot. Sausage can be cooked ahead and gently reheated in a 300-degree oven or a microwave.

15 PATTIES OR ABOUT 1 POUND BULK SAUSAGE

Sage, Thyme, and Apple Sausage

This sausage is truly terrific—slightly sweet and very moist. If you can find it, use ½ pound each of ground turkey breast and ground turkey thighs. When cooked as patties, these are wonderful with the Sage Buttermilk Biscuits (page 24). Dried apples can be bothersome to mince by hand; use a food processor if possible. If not, you may find it easier to lightly oil your knife first. Grate the fresh apple in a food processor or on the large holes of a box grater.

1. In a medium bowl, with a rubber spatula stir together the sage and thyme leaves, turkey, salt, dried and grated apples, cinnamon, and maple syrup.

2. If you want to make patties, form the mixture into 20 3-inch patties.

3. Heat the oil in a large skillet over medium heat. For patties, cook on each side about 3 to 4 minutes, until golden and cooked through; for bulk sausage, simply cook, stirring often, until cooked through and no longer pink.

4. Serve hot. Sausage can be cooked ahead and gently reheated in a 300-degree oven or a microwave.

20 PATTIES OR 1 ½ POUNDS BULK SAUSAGE

2 teaspoons minced sage leaves

1 tablespoon minced thyme leaves

1 pound ground turkey

2 teaspoons coarse salt

½ packed cup dried apples, minced

1 small cooking apple, such as Granny Smith, peeled and grated

Pinch of ground cinnamon

1 tablespoon maple syrup

1 tablespoon canola or olive oil, or more as needed

Cilantro Sausage and Egg Puff

Some variation of this always seems to turn up at church breakfasts, and no wonder—it's

satisfying and easy. Often, though, it's quite greasy, with both pork sausage and lots of cheese;

here, the turkey sausage tones that down a bit. Just remember to prepare the puff the night

before you want it.

9 slices white bread (about 9 ounces), cut into 2-inch cubes

1 pound bulk Cilantro Turkey Sausage (page 118), cooked and crumbled

2½ cups milk

¾ teaspoon coarse salt

6 eggs

¼ teaspoon dried mustard

1¾ cups grated Monterey Jack cheese (about ¾ pound)

GARNISH

Minced cilantro leaves

1. Lightly grease a 9-by-13-inch pan. Spread bread cubes in pan and top with cooked sausage.

2. In a medium bowl, thoroughly whisk together milk, salt, eggs, and mustard. Pour over sausage. Sprinkle evenly with grated cheese.

3. Cover pan with foil and refrigerate overnight.

4. To cook, turn oven to 325 degrees (do not preheat). Remove foil from pan and place in cold oven. Bake about 1 hour, until puffed and golden. Serve hot, garnishing the plates with cilantro.

6 TO 8 SERVINGS

Grilled Tomatoes

These are so easy they really don't require a recipe, but here it is just in case. I usually make them on a stove-top grill or under the broiler. Many herbs will work here—for example, try basil, chives, chervil, dill, or oregano.

1. Heat a grill, stove-top grill, or broiler to a medium-high heat. Sprinkle cut side of tomatoes with olive oil, salt, and pepper. Grill cut-side down, or broil cut-side up, until tomatoes are softened and just starting to char. Sprinkle with herb leaves and bread crumbs if desired (if broiling the tomatoes, there's no need to toast the crumbs first; simply add them and quickly run under the broiler). Serve hot.

1 SERVING (INCREASE AS NEEDED)

1 small tomato or 2 small plum tomatoes, halved lengthwise

1 teaspoon olive oil

Coarse salt and freshly ground black pepper to taste

½ to 1 teaspoon minced herb leaves, such as thyme

1 tablespoon toasted bread crumbs (optional)

Sage-Roasted Potatoes

Based on a recipe from *Cook's Illustrated* magazine, these potatoes stay creamy on the inside while acquiring a crisp crust. If your oven has a convection fan, try using it after removing the foil; it helps in crisping the crusts. I especially like these made with Yukon Gold or other buttery potatoes.

2 tablespoons plus 2 teaspoons minced sage leaves

2 tablespoons olive oil

2 pounds Yukon Gold or red potatoes, unpeeled, each cut into about 8 wedges

1 teaspoon coarse salt, or more to taste

½ teaspoon freshly ground black pepper

2 teaspoons water

1. Preheat oven to 450 degrees.

2. In a large bowl, stir together 2 tablespoons sage leaves and oil, potatoes, 1 teaspoon salt, and pepper until potatoes are coated. Pour water into a shallow pan or baking sheet and top with potatoes, spreading them out evenly. Cover pan tightly with aluminum foil. Roast potatoes for 15 minutes.

3. Remove foil; roast potatoes 15 minutes more. With a metal spatula, turn potatoes over. Roast 10 to 15 minutes more, until cooked through and crisped. Serve hot, sprinkling with remaining sage leaves and more salt as desired.

4 SERVINGS

Ham and Cheese Breakfast Fondue

Here's something different and easy for brunch, and it's great for kids, who always seem to love dipping their food. Take me seriously when I say to add the cheese slowly, making sure each handful is melted—you'll just get one big lump otherwise.

1. In a fondue pot or medium saucepan over medium-high heat, bring cider barely to a simmer.

2. Meanwhile, toss cheese and thyme leaves with flour. When cider is hot, reduce heat to medium and add a handful of cheese. Stir constantly with a wooden spoon or whisk until cheese is melted. Add another handful of cheese, stirring until melted; continue to add remaining cheese slowly, making sure each addition is melted before adding more. Stir in ham.

3. Place fondue pot in base over a low flame (or transfer small amounts of fondue at a time from saucepan to a serving bowl; keep remaining fondue warm). Serve immediately, letting diners use fondue forks to spear the bread and apples and dip into the fondue (remind them to dip deeply to pick up ham pieces). Stir occasionally during the meal to be sure cheese doesn't stick.

6 SERVINGS

1⅔ cups apple cider or juice

1 pound cheddar cheese, preferably extra-sharp, grated

2½ tablespoons minced thyme leaves

2 tablespoons flour

2 thin slices ham (about ¼ pound), diced

ACCOMPANIMENTS

1 loaf French bread, torn into bite-size pieces and heated in a 350-degree oven until crisp; 3 apples, cored and sliced

French-Toasted Breakfast Sandwiches

Easy but different, these sandwiches work well both as a breakfast on-the-go and as an interesting brunch dish. My sister created an hors d'ouevre once of miniature cornmeal muffins filled with rosemary butter, smoked turkey, and cranberry relish; I've stolen most of that idea for these. I especially like the puffy crunch of the bread; just be sure to serve them immediately to retain that crunch. If you can't find the cranberry relish, use well-drained whole-berry cranberry sauce instead.

1 egg

2 tablespoons unsalted butter, melted

¾ cup milk

⅓ cup all-purpose flour

¼ teaspoon coarse salt

2 tablespoons plus 2 teaspoons unsalted butter, softened

2 tablespoons minced rosemary leaves

8 slices firm sandwich bread, such as Pepperidge Farm

4 medium-thin slices smoked turkey

½ cup cranberry–orange relish

1. In a shallow bowl (such as a pasta bowl) or pie pan, thoroughly whisk together egg and melted butter. Whisk in milk, then whisk in flour and salt. Set aside.

2. In a small bowl, mix together 2 tablespoons softened butter and rosemary leaves with a rubber spatula or wooden spoon. Brush 4 slices of bread with rosemary butter, then top each with a slice of turkey. Spread turkey with cranberry relish, then top with remaining 4 slices of bread.

3. Heat a large skillet or griddle, preferably cast iron, over medium heat. Soak sandwiches in egg mixture for 30 seconds per side; while sandwiches soak, melt remaining 2 teaspoons butter in skillet. Transfer sandwiches to skillet and cook for about 1 minute 45 seconds, until golden and crisp; flip and cook about 1 to 3 minutes more, until golden and crisp. (You may need to do this in 2 batches.) Serve immediately.

VARIATION: HAM AND CHEESE BREAKFAST SANDWICHES

1. Omit 2 tablespoons softened butter; stir rosemary leaves into ⅔ cup grated Gruyère or Swiss cheese and divide among 4 slices of bread. Substitute ham slices for turkey; omit cranberry relish. Continue as above.

4 SERVINGS

Soup

for

Breakfast

Lime Basil, Coconut, and Blueberry Soup

Based on a recipe I developed for an article in *Veggie Life* magazine, this soup is pretty and easy, and can be made several days ahead. Coconut milk (found in the supermarket with Thai or Chinese ingredients or other canned milks) is available in a "lite" version, and this is what I use—the fat content of regular coconut milk can be frightening. Cool the cooked blueberries for several hours in the refrigerator, or submerge the saucepan up to its rim in a larger bowl of ice water to cool it quickly.

1 pint fresh blueberries or 1 16-ounce bag frozen blueberries (unthawed)

½ cup granulated sugar

Water: ¼ cup with frozen blueberries, ½ cup with fresh blueberries

3 tablespoons (packed) whole lime basil leaves

1 14-ounce can coconut milk

GARNISH

⅓ cup lightly toasted flaked coconut; 1 tablespoon minced lime basil leaves

1. In a medium saucepan over medium-high heat, bring blueberries, sugar, and water to a boil. Reduce heat to medium-low and simmer berries for 10 minutes, stirring occasionally. Remove from heat and cool.

2. Place blueberry mixture, lime basil leaves, and coconut milk in a blender. Blend on high speed until smooth. Chill, covered.

3. To serve, ladle soup into small serving bowls; sprinkle with coconut and minced lime basil leaves.

4 SERVINGS

Lemon Mint–Cherry Chilled Soup

This soup works equally well with fresh or frozen cherries; I use frozen ones most often. To chill it quickly, put soup in a bowl set over a larger bowl of ice water.

1. Halve 1 cup of the cherries; set aside. In a food processor or blender, puree remaining cherries with sugar, lemon mint leaves, and vanilla until smooth. Add yogurt and pulse until it is just blended in. Taste; add lemon juice if flavor seems flat. Stir in reserved cherries. Chill, covered.

2. To serve, ladle into small bowls; drizzle with vanilla yogurt.

2 TO 3 SERVINGS

¾ pound fresh sweet cherries, pitted, or 1 16-ounce bag frozen sweet cherries, thawed and drained

¼ cup granulated sugar

1 tablespoon (loosely packed) whole lemon mint leaves

½ teaspoon vanilla extract

1 cup vanilla yogurt

1 tablespoon fresh lemon juice if needed

GARNISH

Vanilla yogurt, whisked smooth

Lemon Basil–Blackberry Soup with Basiled Nectarines

As noted in other recipes with blackberries, I resort to frozen blackberries routinely, as fresh can be hard to find. A bag of them works fine here; just be sure they are thawed and drained well. With either fresh or frozen, taste them first; if they're pleasantly sweet, use the lower amount of sugar in the soup.

BASILED NECTARINES

2 small nectarines, diced

2 tablespoons granulated sugar

1½ teaspoons minced basil leaves

1 teaspoon fresh lemon juice

SOUP

¾ cup water

⅓ to ½ cup granulated sugar

3 tablespoons (packed) whole lemon basil leaves

2 cups blackberries

½ cup buttermilk

GARNISH

Whole lemon basil leaves

1. Prepare nectarines: In a small bowl, stir together nectarines, sugar, basil leaves, and lemon juice. Set aside, covered, to macerate while you prepare the soup.

2. Make soup: In a small saucepan over medium-high heat, bring water, sugar, and lemon basil leaves to a boil; boil 1 minute. Cool (to cool quickly, submerge the saucepan to its rim in a larger bowl of ice water; stir frequently). Transfer to a blender or food processor. Add blackberries, and puree. Rub through a sieve to remove seeds. Whisk in buttermilk; chill, covered. (I chill this quickly over a bowl of ice water.)

3. To serve, put a small mound of nectarines in each serving bowl; pour soup around fruit. Garnish with lemon basil leaves.

2 TO 3 SERVINGS

Marjoram, Papaya, and Passion Fruit Soup

I know marjoram seems odd with sweet fruits, but it adds a pleasant spiciness and undertone to this super-smooth soup. The kiwi pieces, with their small seeds, add a little crunch and color. Look for the fruit nectars in the ethnic-foods aisle of your supermarket, or at health food or gourmet groceries. To chill soup quickly, set it over a larger bowl of ice water.

1. Cut a small slice off the top and bottom of each kiwi. Insert a spoon gently just under the peel (with the inside of the spoon bowl facing kiwi flesh), then rotate kiwi to dislodge peel. Cut kiwis into ¼-inch cubes. Cover and chill.

2. In a blender or food processor, puree papaya nectar, passion fruit juice, and marjoram leaves until leaves are minced. Add yogurt and process until mixed (if mixture won't fit in blender or processor, pour into a bowl and thoroughly whisk in yogurt). Serve immediately, or chill, covered.

3. To serve immediately, stir in kiwi cubes; if mixture has been chilled, whisk it to blend again (it may have separated), then stir in kiwi cubes. Ladle into small bowls and float whole kiwi slices on top.

4 TO 6 SERVINGS

6 ripe kiwis

1½ cups (12 ounces) papaya nectar, preferably chilled

2 cups passion fruit juice or nectar, preferably chilled

1½ tablespoons (loosely packed) whole marjoram leaves

1 cup vanilla yogurt

GARNISH

Thin, round kiwi slices (optional)

Cucumber–Dill Soup

This has long been one of my favorite soups; it may be a little jarring to have a savory soup for breakfast, but it will definitely feel right by brunch. Creamy and flavorful, this soup also tastes more complex than it is. Any kind of cottage cheese will do; I prefer a low-fat, but not nonfat, version. Serve this in small dainty bowls, or in large soup bowls, as desired.

2 large cucumbers, peeled

3 cups (24 ounces) cottage cheese

2 tablespoons Dijon mustard

1 tablespoon fresh lemon juice, or as needed

10 chive stalks

¼ cup (packed) whole dill leaves

1 ½ cups milk

Coarse salt to taste

Freshly ground black pepper to taste

GARNISH

Dill sprigs; chopped chives (optional)

1. Halve the cucumbers lengthwise; pull the tip of a spoon down the center of each half to remove the seeds. Cut each half into 4 pieces; place in a food processor or blender.

2. Add cottage cheese, mustard, 1 tablespoon lemon juice, chives, and dill leaves. Process until mixture is smooth.

3. Add milk, salt, and pepper; process briefly to combine (if this won't fit in processor or blender transfer the cottage cheese mixture into a bowl and thoroughly whisk in milk, salt, and pepper). Taste; adjust lemon juice, salt, and pepper as needed. Serve immediately, or chill up to 1 week. To serve, pour into small or medium bowls and garnish as desired.

6 ½ CUPS

Final

Touches

Tarragon Strawberry Sauce

This recipe doubles easily and can be made ahead; reheat over low heat, stirring often. Taste your strawberries as you slice them; if they're not very sweet, increase the sugar by 2 tablespoons.

1 pound fresh
   strawberries,
   sliced, or 20
   ounces frozen,
   sliced strawberries

¼ cup granulated
   sugar

1 tablespoon
   cornstarch

1½ tablespoons
   minced tarragon

1 teaspoon fresh
   lemon juice

1. Toss fresh strawberries with sugar and let stand at least 30 minutes (if using frozen, simply let strawberries thaw in a strainer set over a bowl, then stir in sugar). Drain and reserve juice from berries; add enough water to juice to equal 1½ cups liquid.

2. In a medium saucepan, whisk together strawberry juice and cornstarch until smooth; whisk in tarragon. Cook over medium heat, whisking, until juice is lightly thickened. Remove from heat and whisk in lemon juice. Stir in strawberries. Serve warm; or store, covered, in refrigerator.

VARIATION: CINNAMON BASIL–STRAWBERRY SAUCE

Omit tarragon; stir in 1 tablespoon minced cinnamon basil leaves with the strawberries.

3 CUPS

Blackberry–Thyme Sauce

Where I live, fresh blackberries can be hard to come by, and their season is always too short.

Frozen blackberries will work fine here; in a pinch, even canned and drained berries will do.

This makes a thin sauce. If you prefer it a little thicker, first whisk 2 teaspoons cornstarch into

the water.

1. In a medium saucepan over medium-high heat, stir together 1 cup blackberries and thyme leaves, sugar, and water; bring to a boil. Reduce heat to medium and simmer mixture for 5 minutes. Remove from heat; stir in lemon juice and remaining 2 cups blackberries. Serve immediately, or store, covered, in refrigerator.

3 CUPS

3 cups blackberries, divided

2 teaspoons minced thyme leaves

⅓ cup granulated sugar

¾ cup water

1 tablespoon fresh lemon juice

Lemon Thyme–Raspberry Syrup

This is a fresh-tasting syrup that pairs well with the Raised Lemon Balm Pancakes (page 78).

Make it with either fresh or (thawed) frozen raspberries; it doubles easily. It's also great over

ice cream.

2 cups raspberries, divided

1 tablespoon minced lemon thyme leaves

1 tablespoon granulated sugar

½ cup water

1 tablespoon fresh lemon juice

¼ cup honey

1. In a medium saucepan over medium-high heat, bring 1 cup raspberries and lemon thyme leaves, sugar, and water to a simmer. Boil gently for 5 minutes; remove from heat.

2. Whisk in lemon juice and honey; gently stir in remaining raspberries. Serve warm over pancakes or waffles. Keep leftovers in an airtight container in the refrigerator.

1 ¼ CUPS

Herb Honey

Flavoring honey with herbs is easy and delicious; the honey is good on biscuits or waffles, and as a flavor boost in recipes calling for plain honey. Start with a straightforward light honey, such as clover; save fancier, stronger-flavored honey for other uses.

1. In a small saucepan over medium heat, whisk together honey and herb leaves. Bring just to a boil; remove from heat and let stand 10 to 20 minutes.

2. Pour honey through a strainer (gently reheat it if it became too thick to pour), pressing down on herb leaves in strainer with the back of a spoon or spatula to extract their flavor. Store in an airtight container up to 1 week.

¾ CUP

¾ cup honey

1 of the following herbs:

⅓ cup chopped sage leaves

or ½ cup chopped basil or cinnamon basil leaves

or ⅓ cup chopped tarragon leaves

or ¼ cup dried lavender

or ¼ cup chopped rosemary leaves

or ¼ cup chopped savory leaves

or ⅓ cup chopped thyme or lemon thyme leaves

Chocolate, Cranberry, and Lavender Cream Cheese Spread

Although I expected this to be good, since it was inspired by the fabulous combination of ingredients in my yeast bread (see page 60), this spread surprised me with its addictiveness. Sweet but slightly tangy, and exceptionally creamy, it's great on bagels.

¼ cup semisweet chocolate chips

1 teaspoon dried lavender, or 2 teaspoons fresh lavender, minced

4 ounces cream cheese, softened

½ cup dried cranberries

1. Melt chocolate chips in a double boiler set over, but not touching, barely simmering water, stirring until smooth. (Or place chips in a microwave-safe bowl and heat for 30 seconds on low power; stir; heat again for 15-second intervals as needed until melted and smooth.) Set aside to cool slightly.

2. In a medium bowl with a mixer on high speed, beat lavender and cream cheese until very smooth and fluffy, scraping down sides of bowl with a rubber spatula at least once. Beat in cranberries and melted chocolate just until combined. Serve immediately, or store in an airtight container in the refrigerator.

1 CUP

Pineapple Mint and Basil Ricotta Spread

Try this on bagels, as a crepe filling, or on toast. If you don't have pineapple mint, proceed without it or replace it with ¾ teaspoon peppermint leaves. When draining the pineapple, press down on it slightly to remove excess juice.

1. In a food processor, puree ricotta cheese, sugar, vanilla, and basil and pineapple mint leaves until smooth. Transfer to a medium bowl; stir in pineapple.

2. Store, tightly covered, in the refrigerator for up to 1 week.

2 CUPS

1 15-ounce container low-fat or full-fat ricotta cheese

⅓ cup granulated sugar

½ teaspoon vanilla extract

2 tablespoons (loosely packed) whole basil leaves

1 ½ teaspoons (loosely packed) whole pineapple mint leaves

1 8-ounce can crushed pineapple, drained well

Lavender Blackberry Jam

Although I have made jam the traditional way, using a big canning kettle to process the mixture, I don't often have the patience to do that. So a quick microwave jam comes in handy—friends will be impressed, and you can play endlessly with the flavor combinations. Just don't be surprised if your jam doesn't take exactly the same time as the recipe says, as microwaves can vary considerably.

1 12-ounce bag frozen blackberries, thawed and drained

½ cup apple juice

1 teaspoon dried lavender

½ cup granulated sugar

1. Place blackberries, apple juice, lavender, and sugar in a food processor or blender; process just to coarsely puree the berries. Transfer to a shallow 2-quart baking dish. Microwave, uncovered, on high power for 8 minutes. Stir, then continue microwaving in 5-minute intervals, stirring after each, until jam is thickened—about 20 minutes total.

2. Transfer jam to a very clean, airtight container and refrigerate for up to 3 weeks.

ABOUT ¾ CUP

Strawberry—Mint Preserves

I prefer lemon mint with this, but many mints will do—try orange mint or even chocolate mint. Be sure to stir frequently to keep the preserves from burning. If your strawberries are quite sweet, cut the sugar to 3½ cups; add more lemon juice if needed to balance the flavor (be sure not to burn your tongue when tasting the hot preserves).

1. In a deep pot (such as a stockpot), stir together strawberries, water, and sugar over medium-high heat until mixture comes to a boil. Reduce heat to medium and simmer mixture for about 30 minutes, until somewhat thickened, stirring frequently with a wooden spoon to keep it from burning. Preserves will thicken further upon chilling.

2. Remove from heat; stir in lemon juice and mint leaves. Taste, and add more lemon juice if needed, but be aware that the preserves will taste less sweet when cold. Pour into very clean jars or plastic containers and chill immediately; refrigerate for up to 4 weeks.

4 CUPS

2 pounds fresh strawberries, stemmed and halved (or sliced if large)

⅓ cup water

4 cups granulated sugar

2 teaspoons fresh lemon juice, or more to taste

2 teaspoons minced lemon mint leaves

Rosemary Orange Curd

This curd is based on a low-fat lemon curd recipe by Susan Purdy, which I love for its light texture and less-cloying flavor than standard curd recipes (it's less gooey, more pudding-like than jarred curds). It's wonderful on biscuits and fruit; try it also on the Sweet Orange, Rosemary, and Cranberry Bread (page 58). If this makes more than you want, cut the recipe in half, using ⅓ cup each sugar and orange juice.

1 ½ teaspoons whole rosemary leaves

¾ cup granulated sugar

2 tablespoons cornstarch

¼ teaspoon coarse salt

½ cup hot water

¾ cup fresh orange juice

½ cup heavy cream

1. In a food processor or blender, whiz rosemary leaves and sugar until finely ground. Transfer to a small saucepan and whisk in cornstarch and salt. Whisk in hot water and orange juice. Place over medium heat and bring to a boil, whisking constantly; boil 1 minute, whisking, until mixture is clear and thickened (it will thicken much more upon chilling). Remove from heat and whisk in cream.

2. Press curd through a strainer into an airtight container to remove rosemary leaves. Cover and chill up to 3 days (after which it is still safe to eat, but will be slightly watery; pour off any excess liquid).

1 ¾ CUPS

Lemon Thyme Curd

Another wonderful topping, this curd doesn't require a food processor or blender. Try it on fruit or biscuits, or for a special treat, with the Lemon Thyme Brioches à Tête (page 66). Like the previous recipe, this is more pudding-like than jarred curds. If this makes more than you want, cut the recipe in half, using ⅓ cup each sugar and lemon juice.

1. In a small saucepan, whisk together lemon thyme leaves, sugar, cornstarch, and salt. Whisk in hot water and lemon juice. Place over medium heat and bring to a boil, whisking constantly; boil 1 minute, whisking, until mixture is clear and thickened (it will thicken much more upon chilling). Remove from heat and whisk in cream.

2. Press curd through a strainer into an airtight container to remove lemon thyme leaves. Cover and chill up to 3 days (after which it is still safe to eat, but will be slightly watery; pour off any excess liquid).

1 ¾ CUPS

2 tablespoons chopped lemon thyme leaves

¾ cup granulated sugar

2 tablespoons cornstarch

¼ teaspoon coarse salt

½ cup hot water

¾ cup fresh lemon juice

½ cup heavy cream

Compound Butters

This isn't something you need a recipe for, just general guidelines. Compound butter is simply butter mashed together with a flavoring; you can use one herb or many, as desired. Keep it savory, or make a slightly sweet butter with a little sugar or honey. Compound butters are a good place to showcase delicate herbs whose flavors get lost in cooking, and a good place to test herb combinations. Use a pat of compound butter on breads, waffles, and pancakes; stirred into grits; or as a final dollop of flavor on omelets. Leftover savory butters will find all sorts of uses at dinner as well, such as dill butter on salmon or rosemary butter on steak.

½ cup (1 stick)
  unsalted butter,
  softened

2 to 4 tablespoons
  minced herb leaves

Coarse salt as desired

Freshly ground black
  pepper as desired

1. With a mixer or a wooden spoon, beat together the butter and 2 tablespoons of herb leaves. Taste and adjust flavor with more herb leaves and salt and pepper as desired.

2. Pack into a small ramekin to serve casually, or form into a log: Place the butter in a line down a sheet of waxed paper and use the paper as a guide to shape a log. Roll it up in the waxed paper and chill; slice into thin pats to serve.

½ CUP

TRY THESE HERB COMBINATIONS
  Lemon basil and lime basil
  Salad burnet and dill
  Salad burnet and chives
  Salad burnet, thyme, and marjoram
  Chervil, chives, and tarragon

Chives, marjoram, and savory
Chervil and parsley
Basil and rosemary
Basil, marjoram, rosemary, and thyme
Rosemary, sage, and marjoram
Savory and thyme
Lemon balm and lemon verbena
Lemon verbena and lemon thyme

Menu Ideas

QUICK BREAKFASTS AT HOME
Lime Basil, Coconut, and Blueberry Soup
Chocolate–Lime Crumbcakes

Orange Mint–Banana Frappe
Banana Mint Bread *or* Banana–Basil Oatmeal Sandwich Cookies

Sambuca Latte
Tarragon Chocolate Puffs

BREAKFASTS ON THE GO
Lemon Verbena–Strawberry Smoothies
Lemon Verbena–Blueberry Muffins

Raspberry–Mint Cooler
Orange Mint–Chip Scones

Marjoram, Papaya, and Passion Fruit Soup
Granola Bars

EASTER BRUNCH
Lemon Verbena Lemonade
Roasted Vegetable Galette
Smoked Cheddar and Chive Grits
Lemon Thyme Cream Biscuits
Layered Fruit Salad
Fruited Lemon Biscotti

THANKSGIVING BREAKFAST

Herb Tea
Quick Quiche
Sage Honey–Glazed Sautéed Pears
Sage Buttermilk Biscuits

BREAKFASTS IN BED

Orange Mint–Banana Frappe
Lemon Verbena–Poppy Seed Cakelets
Layered Fruit Salad

Minted Hot Chocolate
Cinnamon Basil French Toast
Baked Pineapple with Basil

Sambuca Latte
Raised Waffles with Tarragon Strawberry Sauce
Allspice Applesauce

REDUCED-FAT BREAKFASTS

Lemon Mint–Orange Cooler
Raised Lemon Balm Pancakes with Lemon Thyme–Raspberry Syrup

Herb Tea
Cinnamon Basil French Toast
Allspice Applesauce

Lemon Verbena Lemonade
Granola (with allspice or basil), with vanilla yogurt

Peach and Pineapple Sage Smoothies
Toast from Orange–Thyme Oatmeal Batter Bread
Rhubarb, Blueberry, and Orange Compote

BREAKFAST FOR SUPPER

Herbed Mushroom Omelet
Grilled Tomatoes
Sage-Roasted Potatoes

Sage, Smoked Cheddar, and Apple Omelet
Smoked Cheddar and Chive Grits
Sage Buttermilk Biscuits

RELAXING BRUNCHES

Herb Tea
Cilantro Sausage and Egg Puff
Sage-Roasted Potatoes
Grilled Tomatoes

Sweet Iced Tea
French-Toasted Breakfast Sandwiches
Layered Fruit Salad
Fruited Lemon Biscotti

Unsweetened Iced Tea with Herbed Sugar Syrup
Ham and Cheese Breakfast Fondue
Banana–Basil Oatmeal Sandwich Cookies

BREAKFASTS TO KEEP YOU WARM

Bay Rice Pudding with Granola Topping
Sage Honey–Glazed Sautéed Pears

Herb Tea
Chocolate, Cranberry, and Lavender Bread Pudding
Lavender Sautéed Apples

Sambuca Latte
Pecan–Banana Bread Pudding
Lavender Sautéed Apples

Sage, Thyme, and Apple Sausage in Sage Buttermilk Biscuits
Smoked Cheddar and Chive Grits
Grilled Tomatoes

Quick Quiche
Havarti–Dill Grits
Apple–Sage Muffins

BREAKFASTS FOR SUNNY DAYS

Lemon Verbena Lemonade
Lemon Basil–Blackberry Soup with Basiled Nectarines
Lemon Thyme Cream Biscuits

Raspberry–Mint Cooler
Sweet Orange, Rosemary, and Cranberry Bread with Rosemary Orange Curd

Lemon Mint–Cherry Chilled Soup
Triple-Lemon Scones with Lemon Thyme Curd

Orange Mint–Banana Frappe
Fruit Puff Pastries with blueberries and mint
Baked Pineapple with Basil

Lemon Verbena Lemonade
Cornmeal Crepes with Lemon Verbena–Ricotta Filling
Layered Fruit Salad

BIRTHDAY BREAKFAST

Sambuca Latte *or* Raspberry–Mint Cooler
Bay Rice Pudding with Granola Crunch
Layered Fruit Salad
"Dessert": Chocolate–Lime Crumbcakes with birthday candles

A Few Mail-Order Sources

Cathedral Greenhouse, at the Washington National Cathedral, Massachusetts and Wisconsin Avenues, NW, Washington, DC 20016-5098; www.cathedral.org/cathedral; (202) 537-6263. Carries banana mint and many other herbs.

Sandy Mush Herb Nursery, 316 Surrett Cove Road, Leicester, NC 28748-5517; (828) 683-2014. Carries a large selection of herbs.

Well-Sweep Herb Farm, 205 Mt. Bethel Road, Port Murray, NJ 07865; (908) 852-5390. Carries allspice trees and a great selection of herbs.

The Baker's Catalogue, from King Arthur Flour, P.O. Box 876, 135 Route 5 South, Norwich, VT 05055; www.kingarthurflour.com; (800) 827-6836. Carries yeasts, parchment paper, baking sheets, and many other baking supplies.

Bridge Kitchenware, 214 E. 52nd Street, New York, NY 10022; www.bridgekitchen.com; (800) 274-3435 or (212) 838-6746. A restaurant supply company that also sells retail; carries yeasts, parchment paper, and many other baking supplies.

Sweet Celebrations, (800) 328-6722. Carries tartlet pans, madeleine pans, and many other baking supplies.

Index